THE KEY

ALSO BY JAMES N. FREY

The Last Patriot
The Armageddon Game
U.S.S.A.
The Elixir
Circle of Death
The Long Way to Die
A Killing in Dreamland
Came a Dead Cat
Winter of the Wolves
How to Write a Damn Good Novel
How to Write a Damn Good Novel, II

How to Write
Damn Good Fiction
Using the Power of Myth

THE KEY

James N. Frey

ST. MARTIN'S GRIFFIN
NEW YORK

Production Editor: David Stanford Burr
Design by Nancy Resnick

www.stmartins.com

Library of Congress Cataloging-in-Publication Data

Frey, James N.
    The key : how to write damn good fiction using the power of
myth / James N. Frey.
        p. cm.
    ISBN 0-312-24917-6 (hc)
    ISBN 0-312-30052-2 (pbk)
    1. Fiction—Technique. 2. Myth in literature. I. Title.

PN3355.F747 2000
808.3—dc21   00-025606

D 10 9 8 7 6 5

To liza, thanks for all the love and everything

Contents

There is no doubt about it, the moment when the story-teller acquires the mythical way of looking at things, the gift of seeing the typical features of characteristics and events—that moment marks a new beginning in his life. It means a peculiar intensification of his artistic mood, a new serenity in his powers of perception and creation.

—Thomas Mann

For in the history of our still youthful species, a profound respect for inherited forms has generally suppressed innovation. Millenniums have rolled by with only minor variations played on themes from God-knows-when.

—Joseph Campbell,
The Masks of God

THE KEY

Introduction: Why Every Fiction Writer in America Should Read This Book

This book is intended to help fiction writers create myth-based fiction, a type of fiction that has the power to profoundly move a reader.

Myth-based fiction is patterned after what mythologist Joseph Campbell has called the *monomyth*. According to Campbell, the monomyth is structurally a reenactment of the same mythological hero's journey; it is prevalent in all cultures, in every era, from the dim beginnings of human consciousness eons ago to the present. This is how Joseph Campbell broadly outlines the monomyth in *The Hero with a Thousand Faces* (1949): "A hero ventures forth from the world of common day into a region of supernatural wonder: fabulous forces are there encountered and a decisive victory is won: the hero comes back from this mysterious adventure with the power to bestow boons on his fellow man."

Note that the hero, in ancient myths, ventures into *a region of supernatural wonder*. This region is also called "the

Mythological Woods." In modern versions of the monomyth, the Mythological Woods is a strange place to the hero, but is usually not filled with supernatural wonder. The modern hero has no dragons to slay. Still, what happens to the modern mythic hero and the ancient mythic hero is unchanged. In the course of his or her initiation on the mythological journey, the ancient and the modern hero alike dies (symbolically) and is reborn to a new consciousness. The hero, through a series of tests and trials, death, and rebirth, is transformed.

The mythological hero, modern or ancient, is on a journey that involves an outer and an inner struggle. The outer struggle is against fabulous forces in the Mythological Woods, where a victory may be won; the inner struggle is to grow through self-discovery and achieve a transformation of character.

Every great work of fiction has such a transformation. In dramatic terms, this transformation is what Lajos Egri in *The Art of Dramatic Writing* (1946) calls growing from "pole to pole."

I wrote about pole-to-pole growth in *How to Write a Damn Good Novel* (1987) and *How to Write a Damn Good Novel, II: Advanced Techniques* (1994). It is one of the most fundamental of all dramatic principles: a coward finds his courage; a godless man finds God; a crook finds his conscience; an honest man is corrupted. This transformation of character is at the heart of all great dramatic works.

- Ebenezer Scrooge, in *A Christmas Carol* (1843), is transformed from a miser into a Santa Claus.
- Charley Alnut and Rosie are transformed in *The Af-*

rican Queen (1946) from a drunk and a religious
zealot into patriots.

- Humbert Humbert, in *Lolita* (1955), is transformed
  from a man enamored of love into a murderous madman.
- Emma, in *Madame Bovary* (1857), is transformed
  from an adventurous flirt into a suicidal depressive.
- Michael Corleone, in *The Godfather* (1969), at the
  beginning morally opposed to his family's criminal
  activity, is transformed into a crime lord.
- In Victor Hugo's *Les Misérables* (1862), Jean Valjean
  is transformed from a petty crook into a Christ figure.
- In Stephen King's *Carrie* (1973), Carrie is transformed from a wallflower into an avenging angel.
- In *Crime and Punishment* (1872), Dostoyevsky gives
  us Raskolnikov, a cold-blooded killer who finds redemption and is transformed into a Christian saint.
- Henry, the protagonist of *The Red Badge of Courage*
  (1895), is transformed from a coward into a hero.
- Scarlett O'Hara, in *Gone with the Wind* (1936), is
  transformed from a frivolous southern belle into a
  shrewd businesswoman.

In this book you'll learn why this transformation has a profound psychological effect on the reader, how it increases
reader identification with the hero, ties the reader emotionally to the story, and forges an unbreakable bond with the
reader. You'll see, too, how other mythic motifs have been
used in the writing of damn good novels—motifs such as
the descent into hell, the trail of trials, learning the new rules,
and having encounters with the Wise One, the Evil One,

the Goddess, the Earth Mother, the Whore, the Fool, the Woman-as-Whore, and so on. You'll see how Magical Helpers and spirit guides appear in modern literature in the form of computers and scientific gadgets. You'll learn how to think in terms of a hero's journey and his or her initiation. You'll learn how to use mythological motifs and characters that have a powerful and profound psychological impact on your reader that is yet fresh and relevant for today. Most important, you'll learn how to create myth-based stories that are uniquely your own.

Literary critic John B. Vickery has delineated the principles common to myth-based theories of literature. These principles, which all fiction writers should have stitched on their pillows, have been summarized by Raphael Patai (1972) as follows:

- The myth-making faculty is inherent in the thinking process, and its products satisfy a basic human need.
- Myth is the matrix out of which literature emerges, both historically and psychologically. As a result, literary plots, characters, themes, and images are basically elaborations and replacements of similar elements in myth and folktales.
- Myth can provide not only stimulation for novelists, storytellers, dramatists, and so on, but also concepts and patterns that the critic can use in interpreting literary works.
- Literature has the power to move us profoundly precisely because of its mythical quality . . . because of the mystery in the face of which we feel an awed delight or terror at the world of man. To continue

myth's ancient and basic endeavor to create a mean-
ingful place for man in a world oblivious of his presence—this is the real function of literature in human
affairs.

Sounds weighty, doesn't it? Even ponderous. But the techniques and mythic patterns and motifs are not difficult to
learn and can be quickly mastered. What follows is a step-
by-step guide that not only describes and explains the mythic
qualities, but also illustrates exactly how they can be woven
into the fabric of your story.

There are, of course, exceptions to everything said about
myth-based fiction in particular and the principles of fiction
writing in general. In this book, even when it is claimed some
principle or concept is "always" true, it may not be. No matter how "always" true something is in art, there are inevitably
exceptions. Be warned, though, that emulating the authors
who have succeeded with their exceptions is dangerous. Just
because James Joyce or Virginia Woolf can get away with
their exceptions and be heralded as great geniuses doesn't
mean you can. Great geniuses often have huge academic es-
tablishments, avant-garde-promoting, grant-giving founda-
tions behind them, and publishing PR departments with
huge budgets trumpeting their genius to the far corners of
the earth. Chances are, you won't be getting the genius treat-
ment, even if you are a genius. Geniuses are very hard for
editors and critics to champion as a rule until after they are
dead, when their muddled sequels will not be popping up to
make the editor or critic who championed them look like a
fool.

Not all geniuses try to find exceptions to the inherited

forms. Many wise old geniuses think of their genius as the gunpowder and the inherited forms as their cannons. Tolstoy was a master of the mythic form in *Anna Karenina* (1877) and *War and Peace* (1869). He did quite well with his career. So did Jane Austen with *Pride and Prejudice* (1813) and *Northanger Abbey* (1818), to name just two. Joseph Conrad's *Lord Jim* (1900) is a mythic gem. These and thousands of other geniuses have used the monomyth (often without conscious knowledge) to great advantage.

These inherited forms are widely used today. Most novels and almost all films are stories involving heroes who journey into a Mythological Woods. Recent examples are the films *Titanic*, where the Mythological Woods is a sinking ship, and *The English Patient*, where the Mythological Woods is a field hospital in World War II. In *Out of Sight*, based on an Elmore Leonard novel with the same title, the hero is a bank robber who escapes from jail and falls in love with a lady federal marshal, a strange Mythological Woods indeed.

In *Saving Private Ryan*, the Mythological Woods begins on the beaches of Normandy in World War II. *A Simple Plan* is about three friends who find a duffel bag in the snow with four million dollars in it. This changes their world into a Mythological Woods where they will undergo their initiation.

The Mythological Woods is everywhere in modern films, novels, and on TV.

One film with a female hero on a journey of initiation is *Shakespeare in Love*. Her Mythological Woods is the theater, where women are forbidden to go. In *Truth About Cats and Dogs*, a fluffy, fun romance—cartoonish escapism—the woods is simply a deception; the hero pretends to be someone else.

Action-adventure films are almost always hero's journeys and are often huge hits. There's the Star Wars saga, of course, which was written with Joseph Campbell's *The Hero with a Thousand Faces* in mind. The Indiana Jones stories have a lot of the hero's journey in them, as do *Romancing the Stone* and *Jewel of the Nile*. Most of Tom Clancy's books and films are myth based: *Patriot Games* (1992), *A Clear and Present Danger* (1989), *Hunt for Red October* (1984).

In literary fiction, *Cold Mountain* (1997) by Charles Frazier involves a journey home from the Civil War through a Mythological Woods of the war-torn United States. It won the Pulitzer Prize. One of Oprah Winfrey's recent picks was Pearl Cleage's *What Looks Like Crazy on an Ordinary Day* (1999). Here the Mythological Woods is the inner cities of America, where the hero must confront monsters like HIV, drugs, violence, and so on. The Mythological Woods, as long as it is not the hero's world of the common day, can be anywhere.

The Giver (1993) by Lois Lowry, a wonderful young-adult novel, features a Mythological Woods that is all gray, and only the hero can see an occasional patch of color. In another wonderful young-adult novel, S. E. Hinton's *Taming the Star Runner* (1989), the Mythological Woods is a Wyoming ranch. E. L. Konigsburg's young-adult Newberry Medal winner *A View from Saturday* (1998) features four heroes on a journey to win an academic contest.

Everywhere you look, the pattern is the same—this year,

last year, ten years ago, a hundred years ago, a thousand years ago, ten thousand years ago; in genre fiction, mainstream fiction, literary fiction; in films, on TV, in short stories—everywhere, for all times, the pattern remains.

Beware of the Bogus

There is a type of bogus myth-based fiction that uses myth as a referent for an elaborate metaphor, where the novelist picks an ancient myth, usually Roman or Greek, and then writes a modern-day copy, often using the mythological names and places, and encourages the reader to think of the specific myth, say, Sisyphus or Oedipus.

This type of myth-based fiction one might call academic myth-based fiction.

Literary critic John J. White (1972), supporting academic myth-based works, says, "A work of fiction prefigured by a myth is read in such a way that our reactions to character and plot are transformed by an awareness of the mythological precedent . . . preconfigurations arouse expectations in the reader . . . the reader of the mythological novel assumes the role of a detective for whom a trail of allusions—signals or clues—has been laid."

The use of myth in this way is a delight to critics and has created a preconfigured myth industry in academic circles, but it is a perversion of true, dramatic myth-based fiction. A novel that invites the reader to participate in this kind of game is asking the reader to leave the story world of his or her imagination and to enter into a game of guess-where-the-mythological-symbol-is-hiding. It is analogous to the contests they used to run in the Sunday comics where you had to pick out all the things that began with P in the picture. This book will be no help whatever if such fiction is what you want to write.

Academic myth-based fiction is simply a form of "metafiction," which has a high-sounding name but is in reality nothing more than authorial sleight of hand. Metafiction grotesquely turns myth-based fiction into an academic exercise, a parlor game for the well-read classicist. It asks the reader to leave the fictive dream, to exit the story world where fiction can work its magic on a reader, and instead to cogitate, to puzzle over the corresponding icons outside the story. It's a game of *Jeopardy* where there are no trips to Hollywood handed out as prizes.

It's nothing more than a cheap trick.

Dramatic myth-based fiction goes far beyond literal correspondence between a particular ancient myth and a modern story. In modern mythic stories, there is a transformation of the hero through struggle, using myth-based characters and motifs: this is what writing in a mythic form really means. Modern stories created by using the power of the monomyth are completely modern and original. The reader is not required to have read Homer or Aeschylus, and there are no references, implicit or explicit, made to ancient myths.

This book is designed to help you use myth-based fictional techniques, not in some bizarre game of find-the-mythic-reference, but rather in the creation of a contemporary, intensely interesting and gripping work, with a stellar cast of fresh, rounded characters.

1

The Awesome Power of Myth

The Storyteller's Magic

As a storyteller, you practice a kind of magic, the most powerful magic on earth. You are a mythopoet, a maker of myth, and it is myth that consciously and subconsciously guides every human being on this planet, for good or ill.

Bunk, you say. Myths are old and dead and have no meaning to modern man.

Better think again.

Think about communism and its mythology. One-fourth of the people on earth still live under communism, despite the recent changes in Eastern Europe and the former Soviet Union. The communists constructed a mythology that they called "scientific." But as Martin Day in *The Many Meanings of Myth* (1984) points out, "The blissful perfection of its ultimate goal, anarchy, follows the party line of Elysium Islands of the Blest, Valhalla, Utopia, New Atlantis, Erewhon, and the Big Rock Candy Mountain."

Millions of people are being imprisoned and put to death

in the name of the communist myth in Cuba, Serbia, China, and Tibet. And many more will die in its name before the myth is dead and buried.

We in the West, too, have our mythologies. The Free Man, as an example. Think you're a "free" American? Tell it to the IRS.

Happiness is a new Buick, the ad men tell us. Smoking will make you good-looking and bristling with health, they told us for years, and look how many millions believed it! Thousands of deaths a year are caused by smoking in the United States, a catastrophe of epic proportions—yet the Marlboro Man ropes in scores of new smokers every hour. Martin Day concludes that modern man, "shorn of his rhetoric and his pretense," is governed by his mythical dreams just as much as are the "Trobriand Islanders and the Kwakiutl Indians."

Be careful when you say something is "just a myth."

The hundreds of Spanish conquistadors who gave their lives looking for the Fountain of Youth are ample testament to the power of myth. So were the Nirvana-seeking Buddhist monks in Saigon during the Vietnam War who poured gasoline on themselves and set themselves on fire while sitting in the lotus position. So are the screaming teenage girls at a rock concert. All have been swallowed up by mythic images.

Aping the mythic figures of John Wayne, Randolph Scott, and Hopalong Cassidy, young Americans a generation ago headed off to Vietnam to "kick a little ass." The myth of the all-powerful American cowboy hero ran into the brick wall of reality. It's no coincidence that as America came to the realization that the ass-kicking image of itself was false, the popularity of Western films and books collapsed. The myth of the invincible Western hero was dead.

Remember the story of Pandora from Greek mythology? She's the young woman who, out of curiosity, disobeyed a rule from On High and opened a box (some say a jar) she wasn't supposed to open, and in so doing let loose all the evils of the world.

You could search the wide world over, and you wouldn't find a single individual who thinks that the evils of the world can be blamed on poor, maligned Pandora. The old gal is dead now and is dismissed as "just a myth" by every single human being on the planet.

But you will have no trouble at all finding people who believe it is manifestly true that the evils of the world can be blamed on a young woman named Eve, who disobeyed a rule from On High and ate an apple she shouldn't have, and *that* brought evil into the world. To hundreds of millions of true believers, the Adam and Eve myth is absolutely, historically true. Millions of faithful believe it is as true as the fact that the sun shines in the daytime. For them, the Adam and Eve myth is a working myth.

In fact, the church to which I belong teaches that the Adam and Eve story happened to real people, just the way it's set down in the Good Book. In my church, if you dared suggest that the Adam and Eve business in the Garden of Eden was "just a myth" made up to explain the mysterious workings of nature to a primitive people, as is the case with Pandora, you would be hooted down, jeered, and branded a blasphemer; you might even be stoned in the parking lot.

When a myth is believed as true, it's a powerful force.

People have been killing each other over myths and their interpretation since, well, who knows? Probably since before Pandora opened the box and before Eve tasted that juicy red pippin, which, by the way, many scholars now believe was actually a pomegranate.

Hundreds of millions of people in the world believe Muhammad leaped into Heaven, leaving behind a hole in the ground in the shape of a foot where he launched himself. They also believe that if you die in a jihad, a holy war, you go right to Heaven. In fact, millions of eager young men proved the force of the myth by charging machine guns while screaming, "God is great!" in one of the bloodiest wars in human history, the Iranian-Iraqi war of 1980 to 1988, which had 2.7 million casualties, including over a million deaths. To the soldiers who so gleefully martyred themselves, there was no question about it: the Muhammadan myth is manifestly true; Muhammad leaped into Heaven, and you can go there too if you die in a jihad.

Just a myth, you say?

Because of the power of men to create myth, Percy Shelley, the nineteenth-century poet, called poets and fiction writers "the unacknowledged legislators of the world."

When Goethe's *The Sorrows of Young Werther* came out in 1814, it was an instant success. It was the story of a young man so obsessed by an unrequited love that he kills himself— a monomythic story of a hero transformed (albeit in a negative way) by love. Over the next few decades, hundreds of young men were found dead with a pistol in one hand, a love note in the other, and a copy of *Young Werther* in their back pockets.

Just a myth, you say?

When Secretary of the Interior Seward met Harriet Beecher Stowe, author of *Uncle Tom's Cabin* (1852), he said, "So
this is the young lady who started it all." He meant the War
Between the States, of course. Her story, a monomythic
masterpiece, was largely a product of her imagination; it depicted slavery as hell on earth and gave impetus to the ab-
olitionist movement and the already-growing war fever.

So would you say her fantastic creation, which led to one
of the bloodiest wars in history, was *just a myth?*

To say the pen is mightier than the sword is to trivialize
the pen. The pen is far mightier than a sword; it's mightier
than an atom bomb. Mightier than all the atom bombs ever
created.

See Leni Riefenstahl's *Triumph of the Will* (1935), and
you can see the effect of the Nazi myth on its followers.
Myth indeed is a potent force.

You, as a fiction writer, have the pen in your hand. What
you create may have an enormous impact on individuals,
communities, nations, the world—and world history.

The ancient peoples of the world knew the power of the
word. In the Old Testament, the Hebrew Scriptures, God
created the heavens and the earth not by waving a magic
wand, but by speaking words. The ancients believed that
your soul was your breath; that words, created by breath,
came from your soul, from the immortal part of your being;
hence, they were sacred. And powerful.

The Gospel of John in the New Testament begins: *In the
beginning was the Word, and the Word was with God, and the
Word was God.*

And the Word . . . *was God.*
Indeed it was. And still is.

The Evolution of Storytelling

Reflect for a moment on the first storytellers.

Human beings first began to bury objects with their dead—jewelry, weapons, pottery, and so on—around a hundred thousand years ago, the archaeologists tell us. These people must have had some notion of life after death—otherwise, what's the point of throwing perfectly good jewelry, weapons, and cooking pots into a hole in the ground?

No one knows when humans began to speak. Language perhaps started out with nothing more than grunts. It must have developed slowly over untold millennia. But certainly by the beginning of the Stone Age—when people were cooperating in hunting large beasts, making villages, and trading with other tribes or clans—language was probably developed enough for hunters to return from the hunt to tell of the excitement of almost killing the huge, woolly mammoth that got away.

Storytelling perhaps began as tales of hunters and gatherers. It is likely that, as with the hunting and fishing and golfing tales today, things had a tendency to get exaggerated. The imagination begins to take over, and the woolly mammoth starts to breathe fire, and, before you know it, you have dragons, giants, and flying horses. The imagination is indeed a curious and powerful thing.

Try putting a dish towel over your hand, pulling it tight,

and tucking it in under you thumb. Tell a three-year-old that this is "Igor," who's looking for magic apples, and the kid will quickly join in the search. For the child there's not much difference between Igor and the magic of the TV, which brings Bugs Bunny into the living room at the push of a button.

The depth of feeling a child may have toward a character in a story is truly astounding. I've seen my own children cover their ears when I—as the wolf in the story—said, "Little pig, little pig, let me come in, or I'll huff and I'll puff and I'll blooooooooooooow your house in!"

Mythologist Leo Frobenius once related the story of a professor friend of his who, being bugged by his four-year-old daughter, gave her three burned matches to play with, calling them Hansel, Gretel, and the witch, and went back to his scholarly pursuits. A while later, the little girl ran to him, terrified, screaming, "Daddy! Daddy! Take the witch away!"

The primitive storyteller sitting at the campfire at night was creating many scary images for his or her audience. Primitive storytellers, looking into the eyes of their audience, could see them grow large, could see their listeners fall into a trance state as the story was being told. They had a distinct advantage over modern storytellers, who can only see the words on the computer screen and must imagine their effect on the reader.

The power of the storyteller to put a reader into a trance state is the source of the storyteller's magic.

If you were to put electrodes on the head of your reader, you would find that as the reader becomes more and more absorbed into the story world—the fictive dream—the brain waves would actually change, resulting, in effect, in a trance state.

Science has discovered that readers of romance novels produce endorphins in their brains. Endorphins are chemically identical to morphine, an extremely addictive drug. Astonishing as it sounds, the romance reader, in fact, becomes *physically* addicted to romances.

A dope pusher may get hundreds of people addicted. A fiction writer can get them addicted by the millions. The storyteller's magic power is truly immense.

Once upon a time a young lad of my acquaintance was madly in love with a comely lass who had moved from the San Francisco Bay area to Seattle to study the art of dentistry. He stayed behind to pursue his career as a magazine editor. At Christmastime, the lad booked a flight to Seattle to visit the lass. Eager was he to be reunited with his true love. On the way to the plane he stopped to buy a book to read on his journey. He chose Stephen King's *The Different Seasons*. He arrived at the departure gate a little early (being anxious to get his journey under way) and took a seat near the counter to await being called to board. He began reading the novel.

Although but a few feet from the counter, and wide-awake, he did not hear his flight announced, did not notice the throngs of people tramping past him to get onto the plane, did not hear his name being called repeatedly. He missed all this, because Stephen King had cast a spell on him. The lad had become so absorbed into the story world that the real world went away.

Such is the power of storytelling.

Clearly, the early storytellers used the phenomena of the natural world as material for their stories. Why is it, the early Greeks must have wondered, that the laurel tree didn't lose its leaves in winter? The storytellers explained it with a story: Daphne was a fair maid, first love of Apollo, but alas, Cupid had shot her with a negative love arrow, and therefore she could love no man—or god. Apollo pursued her with all his will (a sexual harassment case if ever there was one), and, in her desperation, Daphne prayed to Peneus, the river god, to help her. Peneus changed her into a laurel tree. Since she couldn't be Apollo's wife, he made his crown of her leaves, and decreed her leaves would always be green.

You see, the story explains the phenomenon.

Where do frogs come from? According to Greek myth, Latona was cursed by the goddess Juno and went on the run. Thirsty, she asked some people for water, but she was refused. Latona asked Heaven for help, and the people who denied her water were changed into frogs.

Where does lightning come from? Zeus throwing thunderbolts. Storms at sea? Neptune's wrath. The wind? The enormous snores of a god sleeping in a cave.

To the ancients, stories explained all natural phenomena, from the sun's course in the sky to the genesis of disease. Storytellers had become theologians, priests, and priestesses. In the process, they created not only myths but culture.

And the process has continued to this very day.

The Constancy of Myth from Place to Place, Age to Age

Here's a story you might have heard:

A poor widow sends her young son, Jack, to town to sell their cow. Jack is bamboozled by a stranger into selling the cow for five bean seeds. When he gets home, his mother calls him a fool and tosses the seeds out the window. The next morning there's a gigantic stalk grown into the sky. The lad climbs the stalk and finds a mystical land in the sky. Here Jack meets a fairy who tells him yon castle is really his inheritance from his long-lost father, but is now inhabited by a child-eating giant and his one-eyed wife. Jack goes to the castle and encounters the wife, who shields him from the giant. Jack steals a bag of gold and returns home.

After he and his mother spend the gold (in riotous living in some versions, doing good works in others), Jack, dead broke, returns to the magic land in the clouds and steals a hen that lays golden eggs from the giant and escapes back down the bean stalk. Jack and his mother return to prosperity, but when the hen stops laying, Jack goes back again to snatch a magic harp that plays all by itself. Chased by the giant, Jack scoots down the bean stalk and, to cut off pursuit, chops it down. The giant falls to his death. The music of the magic harp soothes the hen, and it begins laying once again, and everyone lives happily every after.

"The Greeks have this tale," Andrew Lang tells us in *Cus-*

tom and Myth (1941), "the people of Madagascar have it, the Lowland Scotch, the Celts, the Russians, the Italians, the Algonquins, the Finns, the Samoans have it, the Zulus, the Bushmen, Japanese, Eskimos. . . . It is not merely the main features that are the same in most remote parts of the world, but even the details."

Some mythologists claim that a recognizable version of "Jack and the Bean Stalk" appears in every culture on earth.

One of the most interesting aspects of the storyteller's art is that it became the rule that the story be told the same each time. Hence, eons passed with very little change in the stories. If you tell the same story over and over again to children, "Goldilocks and the Three Bears," for instance, you might tire of the same ending. Try changing it. Your young listeners will turn on you. The same, no doubt, was true for the ancients. Stories untold millennia old are repeated today exactly as they've been passed down.

Other myths, legends, and folktales (all of which are the products of storytellers) bear remarkable similarities despite the fact that they appear in different cultures, places, and times.

In fact, they sound like copies of each other. Psychologist Otto Rank noted that "even though widely separated by space and entirely independent of each other," myths "present a baffling similarity or, in part, a literal correspondence." Mythologist Martin Day has found some rather striking similarities in the mythologies of various religions from around the world: "The Meru of Kenya state that their culture hero Mugive led the Meru people out of bondage across a sea that parted for them and eventually brought them to a promised land. Mugive possessed a magic staff and transmitted to the Meru seven commandments vouchsafed to him by God. . . ."

This account almost perfectly matches the account in the Bible where Moses leads his people, the ancient Israelites, out of bondage in Egypt across the Red Sea, which parts for them and brings them to the promised land. He gives them ten commandments vouchsafed to him by God.

Martin Day also observed: "Tahiti myth states that Ta'aroa, the creator-god, put the first man to sleep and then extracted from his body a bone from which Ta'aroa formed the first woman. . . ."

In Genesis, Adam is created by God, who then creates Eve from Adam's rib. Truly amazing, isn't it? Coincidence? Mythologists believe that it is possibly a coincidence, even though the similarities are hard to explain.

Cultural borrowing could explain it, of course. Cultural borrowing is common enough.

Let's take, as an example, the Robin Hood legend.

Tradition has it, mythologist Lord Raglan claimed, that Robin Hood's exploits occurred during the twelfth century. It's usually assumed he was a Saxon who fought against the invading Normans. As we all know, and Lord Raglan in *The Hero* (1936) said, he lived with fellows named William, George, Allen, Gilbert, Little John, and Friar Tuck. None of these names, Lord Raglan claimed, are Saxon, and *little* then meant "mean" or "nasty," and friars did not even arrive in England until 1224. And "Robin" is a form of "Robert," which was not a Saxon name either. *Hood* and *wood*, Lord

Raglan pointed out, are the same word in many English dialects.

And then there's the problem with the longbow, with which, supposedly, Robin and his fellows of Sherwood were proficient. It didn't come to England until the battle at Falkirk in 1298.

So who was Robin Hood in history? Most probably, Lord Raglan said, "he was a holdover pagan god, the star of a May Day celebration called 'Robin Hood's Festival.'" Robin Hood was likely an English version of the French cultural hero Robin des Bois, who was the star of French May Day festivals along with Maid Marian, who was "Queen of May."

An even earlier version of Robin Hood may be that of another legendary character, William Tell, who is credited with feats very similar to Robin Hood's.

An astounding example of the similarity of myths from culture to culture is the myth of the hero king. The broad outline of the common "functions" (as mythologists call the significant parts of a myth, legend, or folktale) compiled by Lord Raglan follows:

1. The hero's mother is a royal virgin;
2. his father is a king, and
3. often a near relative of his mother, but
4. the circumstances of his conception are unusual, and
5. he is also reputed to be the son of a god.
6. At birth an attempt is made, usually by his father or his maternal grandfather, to kill him, but

7. he is spirited away, and
8. reared by foster parents in a far country.
9. We are told nothing of his childhood, but
10. on reaching manhood he returns or goes to his future kingdom.
11. After a victory over the king and/or a giant, dragon, or wild beast,
12. he marries a princess, often the daughter of his predecessor, and
13. becomes king.
14. For a time he reigns uneventfully, and
15. prescribes laws, but
16. later he loses favor with the gods and/or his subjects, and
17. is driven from his throne and city, after which
18. he meets with a mysterious death,
19. often at the top of a hill.
20. His children, if any, do not succeed him.
21. His body is not buried, but nevertheless
22. he has one or more holy sepulchres.

Lord Raglan then goes on to see the points of correspondence between this and actual myths. The winner is Oedipus with 22. Theseus scores 20, Romulus 18, Hercules 17, Perseus 18, Jason 15, Bellerophon 16, Pelops 13, Asclepios 12, Dionysus 19, Apollo 11, Zeus 15. Lord Raglan then compares these to the broad outlines of the biblical heroes. Joseph receives 12 points, Moses 20, and Elijah 9.

Moses, as an example, would be scored like this:

His parents (1 and 2) were of the principal family of the Levites and (3) near relatives; he is (5) also reputed to be the son of Pharaoh's daughter (pharaohs were gods, remember). Pharaoh (6) attempts to kill him at birth, but (7) he's wafted away and (8) reared secretly. We are told (9) nothing of his childhood, but on reaching manhood he (11) kills a man and (10) goes to Midian, where (12) he marries the ruler's daughter. Returning (10) to Egypt he (11) gains a series of magical victories over Pharaoh and (13) becomes a ruler. His rule lasts a long time, and then (15) he flees from leadership and (18) dies on a mountain. His children do not succeed him (20).

The correspondence with the myth of the hero king and the gospel accounts of Jesus Christ is also rather striking. When this fact was first noticed by the Europeans who were colonizing the New World in the sixteenth and seventeenth centuries, it threw them into a panic. How could this be, that the myths of these pagan savages were so close in form and function to the story of Christ? Instead of seeing the similarity as speaking to the universal brotherhood of mankind, these European dimwits went full speed ahead burning books and records and smashing temples and icons, committing the biggest cultural genocide in history.

The Adventures of Mythic Heroes in Modern Times

Here's a familiar story:

A jaded loner of a detective—tough on the outside, soft on the inside—who lives in a trailer, a boat, his office—any place but a house in the suburbs with a wife and kids—is hired by a young woman whose father, uncle, sister, brother, boss, cousin, friend—anyone but a husband—is in mortal danger. The detective reluctantly takes the case, and after a while he finds a body, follows suspects, interviews people who don't seem to know much, is bumped on the head, gets chased; the young woman client is kidnapped, the detective finds the killer, rescues the client, recovers the diamonds, gold, or whatever the bad guys are really after, and in the end the detective brings the bad guys to justice. Oh yes, the detective drives a beat-up Caddy, a Ferrari, a vintage Porsche—anything but a Chevy two-door sedan. In the TV show *Murder She Wrote*, a female version of the same story, the detective hero rides a bike. (For the purposes of this book, a "hero" is not a sex-specific term, so a hero can be either a man or a woman. Fastidious grammarians, please forgive us our trespasses.)

In the male version, the detective is often named after manly things, usually a gun. Peter Gun. Canon. Winchester. Magnum. Have you ever in your life met anyone named "Magnum"? Check the phone book. You won't find a single one.

Anyway, the woman-in-trouble detective story has been told on American television fifty times a week now for fifty years. With reruns, it's up there into the millions of showings to countless billions of people if you count all the stations around the world. You'd think audiences would tire of it. You'd think they'd scream for something different, something fresh, anything. But they don't, and they won't.

The reason is that the TV detective story is mythic, and because it is mythic, the retelling of it confirms its mythic power.

A myth confirms and reconfirms our most deeply held cultural beliefs. The TV detective story confirms our deeply held cultural belief that the *individual* can bring justice to a situation of injustice. We believe deeply in individualism.

There's another oft-told story in America.

An attractive young woman, usually fair-skinned and fair-haired (let's call her Sydney), meets a darker-complected man (let's call him Dirk) a few years older, wiser, and richer, though nowadays she has a career and is usually quite successful, so the attraction isn't purely financial. She finds herself irresistibly (let us say, biologically) attracted to him. The pull is incredibly strong, yet both resist because of objections from the family, society, or whatever. Meanwhile, another character (let's call him Philip) is pursuing the young woman. Philip is perfect: went to all the right schools, has money in the bank, and so on. Sydney's mother thinks he's swell. Meanwhile, Sydney has to deal with Dirk over some problem—his race car is disturbing her bird sanctuary, say—and while they shout over the noise of his throbbing engines, they're becoming more and more irresistibly and profoundly attracted to each other. It's maddening, really. Finally, as Philip gets closer and closer to winning the fair maid, the attraction between Dirk and Sydney becomes so powerful it can no longer be contained. It erupts, and the two lovers throw themselves at each other in a titanic collision of love and sex and all that, and they end up happily in a committed relationship.

This story has been told in romance novels thousands of times. In fact, over half of the novels sold in America (measured in units sold, not dollars) are sold by a single publisher—Harlequin Books of Toronto, Canada—and all of them are a variation on this single theme: love wins out.

Such is the power of myth.

The romance is simply another version of mediaeval romances such as Eloise and Abelard, and more ancient stories, such as Samson and Delilah. Before that there was *The Iliad*, a great love story, which is no doubt a retelling of older myths that go back to the Stone Age. For how many more millennia will the romance formula continue to attract readers? As long as there are men, women, and biology, no doubt.

The myth of the lone detective is an urban version of an older myth, the lone gunman of the Old West, which was an incarnation of the lone gunman on the frontier, and the lone knight errant, who was an incarnation of Ajax and Achilles and Ulysses. This hero is centuries old. In fact, the tough guy–private eye–frontiersman–knight-errant–Greek warrior is older than writing itself. Far older. Uncounted millennia older. Who is this hero? He is a fighter for justice. He has a quick gun or a quick sword, a big fist, a big mouth, and a soft heart.

Two Heroes

Let us consider an ancient hero, Hercules—the Roman name for the Greek hero Heracles. Hercules was the son of the god Zeus and his mistress, the human wife of a Theban general. Hera, Zeus's wife and a goddess, sent two great snakes to kill Hercules while he was yet a child, but the lad was so strong he killed the serpents. As a young man, he

killed a lion with his bare hands. Later, he was to complete
twelve labors, including killing another lion, a twelve-headed
Hydra, and savage birds with bronze beaks. No problem.

Hercules is courageous, tremendously strong, and fero-
cious in battle. And he acts for his people.

Joseph Campbell, in *The Hero with a Thousand Faces*, says
of Hercules:

> He has our sympathy because he performs his he-
> roic deeds for the people.... Secondly in per-
> forming his labors served a master. Thirdly [he
> has] a second in command who stands by his side
> and occasionally even saves his life.... Fourthly,
> and most importantly, there is a feature of inher-
> ent superiority that sets the hero apart from or-
> dinary mortals . . . this superiority is so impressive
> that the cause he represents becomes automati-
> cally right and our total sympathy is immediately
> captured by him.... Herein, precisely, lies the
> basic psychological significance of the [Hercules]
> myth . . . [such heroes] enable us, in fact almost
> compel us, not only to identify with their heroes,
> but to derive deep emotional-moral satisfaction
> from the feats they—and through them, we—
> perform . . . the more familiar the hero, the more
> often we have watched him overcome ever-
> increasing dangers and challenges, the more we
> know what to expect of him, the more we identify
> with him . . . the hero gains immeasurably from
> repetition.

Hercules has immense strength, resourcefulness, ingenuity, stick-to-itiveness, and he is, at times, slightly buffoonish. He also has an insatiable sexual appetite.

Many centuries later, a former British intelligence officer, Ian Fleming, invented the character of James Bond. Bond has immense strength, resourcefulness, ingenuity, stick-to-itiveness, and he is, at times, slightly buffoonish. And he has an insatiable sexual appetite.

It's obvious Bond is not just a hero, but a mythic hero. For one thing, he's surrounded by mythological characters (whom we'll be discussing at length later) such as the "Herald" named M, who brings Bond his mission, and a "Magical Helper," Q, who gives him his magic. Magic, you say? Certainly: a briefcase full of magic in *From Russia with Love* (1957). In later stories he uses folding helicopters, a pen that fires rockets, a personal submarine, and so on.

It's usually a tip-off that a story is myth based when the characters have names like M and Q or numbers, such as "007." Bond is just as much a mythic hero as Hercules, except that he has modern magic: technology. He has his souped-up Astin Martin that fires rockets, he has the exploding briefcase, he has hideaway sniper rifles, and he can call on his Magical Helper Felix of the CIA to give him more magic any time he wants it.

Another way you can tell he's a mythic hero is that he is on the side of good fighting evil. There are no redeeming qualities in James Bond's enemies, such as Dr. No or Goldfinger or any other villains in the *Bondiad*. They are as evil as Grendel, the monster in *Beowulf*; as evil as Prince John and the Sheriff of Nottingham are to Robin Hood; as evil as Circe, the witch, is to Ulysses; as evil as Satan in the Garden of Eden.

Reading about a mythic hero such as James Bond is a confirmation of an article of faith on the part of the reader. Ian Fleming's *Goldfinger* (1959) is just as much a fable as *Jason and the Argonauts.* A fable in modern dress. Most modern mythic heroes are easily recognized as mythic. Dirty Harry, the cops on *NYPD Blue,* all the tough-guy cops from Sam Spade and Mike Hammer to Spenser are little changed from when their names were Sir Lancelot, Ulysses, Samson. The stories about them are incarnations of legends and myths as old as human speech.

It is the thesis of this book that the fundamental mythic storytelling techniques have survived and developed through the millennia and are with us today just as much as they were with ancient man. The hero of popular fiction is the legitimate heir of stories going back untold millennia, and the forms of stories and the cultural ideas that they illustrate are unchanged. If the modern writer is made aware of these forms and the cultural role of myth in the lives of modern man, he or she will be able to use them as a powerful tool that speaks to the reader at the deepest levels of the unconscious mind.

But what if you don't want to write James Bond-type shoot-'em-ups? Can you still use this mythic form if you want to write more-mainstream or even literary fiction?

Of course you can.

A member of my Berkeley workshop, Tess Collins, patterned her hero's journey after the mythic hero, and sold her novel *The Law of Revenge* (1997) for a healthy advance. In the novel, Alma Bashears is a thoroughly modern, successful, and classy San Francisco lawyer who goes home to the hills of Kentucky, where she never intended to return, to defend her brother, accused of murder. Her own childhood hometown has become the Mythological Woods. There she will go through an initiation and be transformed.

Ernest Hemingway's *The Old Man and the Sea* (1952) is a mythic masterpiece. The hero, the old man Santiago, is possessed of great courage and special skills and takes great risks to bring food to his people and to serve as a model and example. He is just as much a hero as Hercules or James Bond. The Nobel Prize committee singled out *The Old Man and the Sea* for specific praise as having lasting literary merit when Hemingway was awarded the prize. In Avery Corman's *Kramer vs. Kramer* (1977), the hero, Mr. Kramer, suddenly finds himself deserted by his wife. He enters the Mythological Woods, where he is given trials, symbolically dies, and is reborn as a responsible father.

One of the biggest commercial hits of the past decade was John Grisham's *The Firm* (1991). In it, the clever and resourceful ambitious yuppie hero, Mitch McDeere, enters the Mythological Woods—he goes to work for a Mafia-owned law firm in Memphis and in the end is transformed, reborn as an island-hopping beach bum in the Caribbean.

Myth and Its Importance to the Fiction Writer

Many theories have been advanced to account for the similarities in myths from around the world. The various theories can be classed as "spread" theories, naturalistic theories, psychoanalytical and mass dream theories (Freudian), and inherited engram theories (Jungian).

The spread theories say it all came about through cultural borrowing, that human culture started in one place, usually someplace in Africa, and spread throughout the world. Others claim it all started in the Garden of Eden. Whichever theory is correct, the point is, as mankind spread from some place of beginning, myths spread as part of cultural baggage. Even though language changed, the myths stayed constant. Such is the power of myth.

Myths also spread through trade and conquest, often with a change of names for the heroes.

The naturalistic theory of why myths are so similar proposes that myths are symbolic representations of natural events. The first to advance this idea was perhaps Max Muller in an essay titled "Comparative Mythology" (1897) and published in book form in 1909. He maintained that myths tell about natural phenomena such as dawn, day, night, and the seasons. Take, as an example, the Oedipus myth. It was foretold by an oracle that Oedipus would kill his father and marry his mother.

Okay, to prevent that from happening, Oedipus leaves Corinth and bumps into his father, whom he doesn't recognize, and they quarrel, and Oedipus kills him. Later, he meets his mother and marries her without recognizing her, quite by accident. But when he finds out what he has done, Oedipus is overcome with remorse and puts out his own eyes, and his mother/wife kills herself. A naturalist would say that Oedipus is the sun, who kills his own father, the darkness; marries his mother, the sky; and dies blinded as the setting sun.

Maybe this does account for some of the similarities. But it certainly is not the full story.

The psychoanalytical school of Sigmund Freud sees myth as a sort of public dream, which reflects an underlying truth about the pyschosexual life of the individual. As an example, the myth of the birth of the hero (a common element of myth is that heroes have a special birth) is a retelling of the birth trauma of every individual, the memory of which is supposedly buried in the subconscious. The pattern of the monomyth is simply a retelling (in the Freudians' view) of the individual's break with the parents and learning to adjust to the demands of the adult world. In other words, every story is a coming-of-age story.

Psychiatrist Carl Jung had a different theory of mythic origins and a different view of the subconscious (which he called "the unconscious") mind from that of Freud. Jung claimed the unconscious was split in two. One half he called the "individual" unconscious, which was pretty much like Freud's, consisting of hidden or repressed memories of bad times, impulses suppressed, and the like. The other half was the "collective" unconscious. In Jung's theory, myth takes a central place. Mythical motifs are structural elements of the psyche, he claimed. He used the term *archetype* to describe the commonly found components of myth.

Jung thought that the components of myth were actually biological structures of the brain—that they are, so to speak, hardwired into a mental computer. Myths, Jung proposed, were automatically responded to upon an individual's hearing them. The individual uses these structures and the myths themselves to help in his or her own transformations. They are patterns of behavior, stored away for future use. When a young woman becomes a bride, a wife, and a mother, she must transform herself. The mythological models in her mind show her the way to accomplish this. Say she decides later to go to medical school. What ordinary person can slice open the skin of another human being and start unfolding the guts inside? One must first be psychologically prepared by going through the initiation rite, the mythic journey of transformation called medical school.

To accomplish any kind of personal change, you will find yourself following the path of the hero of a monomyth.

In the old days, say of the Vietnam era, a young man lounging around his parents' home is suddenly drafted (the call to adventure). He leaves home (crossing the threshold); he gets his hair cut and puts on a uniform (changing his appearance); he learns to fire a rifle, to march, to say, "Yes, sir" (learning the new rules); he must go on long marches and fight (being tested); and somewhere along the line he starts to think of himself as no longer a civilian: he is now a soldier (death and resurrection—the birth of a new individual consciousness), and so on.

The pattern is the same yesterday, today, and tomorrow in the lives of our heroes and our lives as well.

No matter which theory or combination of theories one might believe accounts for the similarity of myths around the world, it doesn't really matter. The fact is, these similarities exist. Somehow, mythic forms resonate in every individual human being on this planet. When a human being encounters some version of a myth, the individual responds at a very deep level, subconsciously, and is powerfully drawn to it as by magic. The force of myth is irresistible. Mythic forms and mythic structures are the foundation on which all good stories are built; these forms and structures are the key a modern fiction writer can use to create powerful fiction.

Mankind's Greatest Achievement

It is often said that the taming of fire is mankind's greatest achievement. Others say it's the invention of the wheel. Both are wrong. Mankind's greatest achievement is the invention of the mythic hero. How exactly this miracle came about no one is sure, but the impact of the hero on society has been momentous.

Let's go back for a moment to the nightly campfire of a primitive tribe in Europe.

The storyteller is telling of the adventures of Beowulf, who, after fighting a monster named Grendel, becomes king, and later fights a dragon to the death.

Beowulf is brave, resourceful, noble, self-sacrificing, per-

forms his deeds for the people, and so on. He's an incarnation of the hero with a thousand faces.

Of course, as the members of a tribe listen to this tale,
they become transfixed. They experience what the hero is
experiencing and succumb to all the usual sympathetic magic
tricks storytellers perform for their listeners. The storyteller
is the tribe's entertainment and creates the mythic pattern of
change for the individuals of the tribe.

The storyteller's stories have become the myths of the
tribe by this time. Beowulf is not just showing us the way to
change, he is a model of behavior. The hero's deeds convey
to members of the tribe how they must act. They, like Beowulf, must be self-sacrificing and brave, fight evil, and so
on. Heroes are our models: their stories convey to each suc-
ceeding generation the cultural values of the tribe.

Samson was a cultural hero to the ancient Israelites. Samson, like Beowulf, is an incarnation of the hero with a thousand faces. He is brave, self-sacrificing, and fights the evil
Philistines. In addition, he has religious significance. He is
a "judge" of Israel. He was dedicated to God when he was
a child, and God has in return given him superhuman
strength.

The story of Samson and Delilah in chapter 16 of the
Book of Judges in the Old Testament of the Bible is the
story of betrayal. First Samson betrays God by becoming an
egomaniac; then he falls in love with Delilah, who betrays
him by cutting off his hair, thus causing him to lose his
strength. He is blinded, chained to a wheel, and mocked,
and then, through facing up to his sins and asking for mercy,
is redeemed by God. Samson is the perfect hero for the

Israelites—not only does he have the usual heroic qualities, but he has a spiritual death and rebirth as well.

So do, of course, many of the Greek heroes. Whereas Israel's heroes must be true to their God and their God alone, and they must obey the Torah, the Greeks, whose religion was a religion of fate, must accept theirs or incur the wrath of the gods.

Today, in America, the God of obedience has become the God of freedom. Our heroes don't follow the law; they can only succeed if they disobey it. Our cultural values are individualist, not tribal. The modern private investigator from Hammet's Sam Spade and Chandler's Philip Marlow to Paretsky's V. I. Warshawski and Grafton's Kinsey Millhone are loners who must break the law—commit break-ins, lie, make forgeries, co-opt other identities, and so on—to bring lawbreakers to justice.

The male hero of the modern romance is very much the same outlaw type, living by his own code at the fringes of society. The modern mystery and the modern romance make up a huge percentage of the fiction sold in America today, perhaps 80 to 85 percent. The millennia-old hero marches on, dressed in a new suit.

Our modern heroes have all the classic qualities of the mythic hero: great strength (mental or physical), great courage, great skill; they're loyal and have sexual magnetism, unrelenting determination to conquer evil, and the assistance of magic or a Magical Helper.

The ancient mythic female hero often took the form of innocence personified. In ancient tales she was in need of rescue by the knight. Later she was the star of the gothic romance, where her innocence was in peril from dark, vaguely evil men with seemingly base desires. In modern times, she's still with us, and though still often somewhat innocent or naive, she is no longer virginal and helpless.

At times, a male hero, too, may be the innocent in peril, as in Bram Stoker's *Dracula*.

The purpose of fiction in general is still, today, essentially religious. What! you say. Religious? That's right, religious. Literature proves there is order in the universe. It says that, in life, moral choices lead to outcomes. In fiction there is meaning in human events. If life is chaos, and literature mirrors this chaos, there's no point to reading. If "stuff happens," but events, choices, and conflict resolution do not lead anywhere, there would be no reason for a reader to read fiction at all. Readers read to be reassured that life does have meaning and there is order behind all the chaos. These are essentially religious sentiments.

There is comfort in reading literature primarily because it proves to us that life matters, that what we do matters. Love can conquer all. Justice will prevail.

Now that we've covered myth in general, it's time to get down to the actual monomyth itself, and how one goes about creating a modern version from the ground up.

2

What It's All About Is Who

A Note About the Design of This Book

In the first part of this book, the part you have read so far, I have offered what I hope is overwhelming evidence that mythic structures, forms, motifs, and characters deeply resonate with the reader. These structures, forms, motifs, and characters are, as the title says, "The Key" to writing more-powerful fiction.

Now it is my intention to show you how to harness that power in your own work.

To do this, I will show the steps that need to be taken in creating a myth-based story, and I will discuss the mythic character types, motifs, and structure as we encounter them during the process of creating the story. The sample story is called *The Blue Light*. The hero and other major characters in *The Blue Light* and in other myth-based stories have certain qualities. These will be discussed, and then a character will be created to show how it is done.

Although variations of the form are common, most myth-based stories will generally follow this pattern:

- A myth-based story begins in the world of the hero's common day, where the hero is found already struggling with common-day problems. This is the part of the myth called the "separation" by Joseph Campbell.
- In the world of common day the hero will receive a "call to adventure," which sooner or later he or she will answer. The call to adventure will require that the hero leave the common-day world.
- Before departing, the hero may get advice from a Wise One, secure weapons from an Armorer, get magic from a Magical Helper, be warned not to go by a Threshold Guardian, have a tearful good-bye with a Loved One, and do other things.
- The hero then crosses a threshold and enters the "Mythological Woods," where the hero will learn the new rules and be tested. This second part of the monomyth Joseph Campbell calls the "initiation."
- During the initiation the hero will have a "death-and-rebirth" experience that will change him or her forevermore.
- As a supreme test during the initiation, the hero will have a showdown with an Evil One where the hero may be killed or may win a prize to bring back to his community as a boon. If the hero is not killed, this begins what Joseph Campbell calls the "return," the third part of the hero's journey.
- The hero will cross another threshold and head home with the prize. Along the way the hero may have

another confrontation with the Evil One and be tested further and may even lose the prize and have to recapture it.

- Upon reaching the world of common day, the hero may be hailed as a hero who brought a valuable prize that will be a boon to his people or be denounced as a villain if the prize is not honored.

I will end the book with a discussion of the comic hero, the tragic hero, and a final example, a short fable.

Okay, let's begin by creating our sample story where writers always begin, with the "germinal idea."

The Germinal Idea

The germinal idea, that first seed, that first hunch that there's something here that may grow into a story, is what sets the creative process in motion. The germinal idea can be anything that gets your creative juices flowing. It can be a place, a person, an odd event. It can be anything that provides the spark that ignites your creative fires.

Here's where I got the germinal idea for *The Blue Light*.

One night I was driving through the desert on Interstate 80 east of Reno, Nevada. I was on a lonely stretch of road, about three in the morning, cruising in my VW Jetta at about eighty miles an hour. Fogged with sleepiness, I was concentrating on trying to keep awake when I glanced to the south and saw a blue light in the sky.

At first I thought it was my blurred vision getting blurrier.

I slowed and kept glancing over at it. It seemed to be corkscrewing its way upward, shimmering and pulsing.

I pulled over to the shoulder and stopped. It appeared to be maybe ten or fifteen miles away, but that was a blind guess—it could have been five or fifty. I got out of the car. It was a starlit night, no moon. The blue light seemed to be doing some kind of weird, slow dance. It reached quite high up, possibly several thousand feet in the air. Then, suddenly, it stopped—blink! as if somebody had turned off the switch. I stood there for several minutes waiting to see if it would come back on, but it didn't.

A trucker had stopped nearby. He looked at me and shrugged his shoulders and got back into the cab of his big rig.

I stopped at the next town, Lovelock, for gas and asked the clerk if he had any idea what the blue light was, and he just smiled and said, "Hey, Nevada is the UFO capital of the planet. Spacemen are probably having a convention up there."

I never did find out what the blue light was. A friend of mine lives in Reno, and he says he never saw anything in the media about it, so what it really was, I have no idea.

Okay, this blue light is my germinal idea for this story. It's a simple idea. There's a weird blue light appearing in the sky. It's a strange, gyrating kind of light, shimmering, pulsing, dancing. It's not a searchlight, not airport lights, not a warning light—nobody knows what it is. It comes and goes. It's like crop circles in the sky, eerie and mysterious. I'm going to create a novel about someone whose life is transformed by the adventure they have investigating this light.

The next step was to figure out what the blue light really

was—what it would be in my story. I kicked the idea around my study for a while, brainstorming like a madman. It could be a real UFO or a secret government project. Or it could be a hoax. I had all kinds of ideas, from space aliens to the Second Coming. Now, I've decided what causes it, but I'm not going to tell for the moment so that when you read the following, you'll be held in suspense just as the reader will be held in suspense. Part of the fun is playing with the reader's mind, eh?

Now that I have my germinal idea, the next step is to figure out who my hero is going to be.

The Qualities of the Hero

The hero of myth-based fiction has certain qualities that attract a reader and will not have other qualities that readers find repellent. These qualities are time-tested. It does not mean that a character who lacks one or more of these qualities would not be an interesting character who would attract a reader. But before you dispense with any heroic quality, you should know that heroic qualities have been proven over several millennia of testing to attract readers like honey attracts bears. If you leave some of these qualities or traits out, it's like leaving out a few spark plugs when you do a tune-up.

In *How to Write a Damn Good Novel* I wrote about creating flesh-and-blood characters who were driven and three-dimensional and had a ruling passion. In *How to Write a Damn Good Novel, II: Advanced Techniques,* I further suggested that fiction writers create characters who are interesting in the sense that real people are interesting, that they have interesting backgrounds and might even be a little wacky. Now I'm advancing the notion that the hero of your myth-based novel should have heroic qualities as well.

There is a danger in creating characters for a novel with mythological motifs and heroic qualities in mind. The author may fall into the trap of thinking all one needs to do is to follow some kind of magical mythic formula full of wooden characters and cliché situations and, voila, a mythic-novel masterpiece pops from your word processor. Nothing could be farther from the truth. The mythic hero needs to be just as three-dimensional, interesting, passionate, and dramatically driven as any other dramatic character. You will need to put more work and care—not less—into the creation of mythologically heroic characters.

The hero, first of all, is an "extreme of type." We are not writing about middle-of-the-roaders when we write myth-based fiction. If we're going to write about a rodeo rider, he's the bronco busting, bull-bareback riding buckaroo of all time. He or she should be larger-than-life, driven, maybe desperate, neurotic, even wacky. Good characters are far-out, and that goes for myth-based fiction as well as dramatic fiction. Make your hero stand out in a crowd.

The hero of a myth-based work of fiction will always possess qualities in addition to being a great dramatic character:

- The hero has courage (or finds it in the course of the story).
- The hero is clever and resourceful.

- The hero has a "special" talent.
- The hero is an "outlaw," living by his or her own rules.
- The hero is good at what he or she does for a living.
- The hero is a protagonist (takes the lead in a cause or action at some point in the story).
- The hero has been "wounded" (maimed, disgraced, grieving for a lost loved one, etc.) or is wounded in the course of the story.
- The hero is motivated by idealism (at least at some point in the story).
- The hero is sexually potent.

Now to discuss each of these qualities individually:

The Hero Has Courage (or Finds It in the Course of the Story)

The reader cannot identify with the hero unless the hero has courage. Heroes may at times refuse to go on a mission, but rarely is it because they lack courage. Readers are repelled by cowards. It's as inborn in the human species as the fear of snakes.

A few years ago I took a class in romance-novel writing given by Phyllis Taylor Pianka. The sixteen women in the class were fledgling writers, but they had all read hundreds, if not thousands, of romance novels. In the class, I read a portion of a romance novel I was attempting to write. In the opening situation, the heroine and her fiancé were going to her aunt's place for a visit. The aunt lived in a spooky old house. The fiancé, as he came to the front stairs, hesitated, looking over the decrepit old Victorian before proceeding.

The class members all said that they knew the fiancé was not the hero of my story. Why? I said. He's handsome, witty, wild about the heroine, educated, successful, and so on, but they all shook their heads. He *hesitated* before going up the stairs. That he lacked courage was a tip-off to them that he was not the hero. You see, the hero does not hesitate unless there's real peril. A spooky old house will not give a courageous hero pause.

There are, of course, many great stories about a cowardly hero finding his courage. In the thirties, forties, and fifties, many Western films were made in which the hero had hung up his gun and now, menaced, is pressured to pick it up again. Usually the hero has not lost his courage in these films but only seems to because he's found religion, or is sick of killing, or whatever. His sweetheart, the townspeople—everyone—think he has turned gutless, but usually the audience knows better. *Shane* is such a film, a classic. At the beginning of the film the hero has hung up his guns; in the end he straps them on again and goes and shoots up the bad guys.

There are other stories, however, in which the hero is a coward at some point in the story. In these cases, that is what the story is about: the hero finding his courage. The hero's struggle to find his courage is the core conflict of such stories.

The Hero Is Clever and Resourceful

For readers to identify with them, heroes must also be clever and resourceful. The reader has no patience, except in comedy, for an inept hero. This is not to say that the hero needs to be a caricature such as an Indiana Jones, with an encyclopedic knowledge of every conceivable subject and a mastery of every possible skill from sausage making to nuclear physics. To be clever and resourceful, a character does not have to have special knowledge. In fact, it often helps the story if your clever and resourceful hero is lacking in the specific skills required by the situation. This is sometimes referred to as the "fish-out-of-water motif."

I remember seeing a very good fifties noir-type film in which a rich man—a rather disagreeable, selfish character—was lured into the desert by his wife and her boyfriend to murder him. They pushed him off a cliff. He wasn't killed, but he broke his leg in the fall. Rather than go to the trouble of climbing down the cliff to finish him off, the would-be killers leave him there to die of thirst.

The hero in this case is a businessman, a city dweller, and has no experience as a survivalist. But he is clever and resourceful. He makes a splint for his leg and fashions a crutch. He figures out that water could be under the sand where he can see it had pooled during the rainy season. In other words, he uses his wits to save himself and is transformed by the experience.

One interesting feature of the hero of that story is that he was not *admirable*. Nor likable. He was a greedy, ruthless businessman, with whom the reader would not ordinarily want to spend an afternoon. But heroes are not required to be admirable or likable. Take the film *Patton*. The Patton character, played brilliantly by George C. Scott, was pretty despicable—a bully, a braggart, flamboyant; a pearl-handled-.45-packing lunatic—but he was fascinating, too. The film was a huge hit.

Many readers find Scarlett O'Hara in *Gone with the Wind* hardly admirable. But she's certainly clever and resourceful. After her father's plantation, Tara, is smashed by the Yankees—her whole way of life destroyed—she manages to rebuild it from the ashes.

A wonderful classic short story by Carl Stephenson, "Leiningen versus the Ants," was made into a gripping film called *The Naked Jungle* (1954) starring Charlton Heston as Leiningen, whose cocoa plantation is being set upon by army ants, the *marabunta*. Leiningen is a pompous jerk. He's arrogant, boastful, full of hubris, and downright nasty to his mail-order bride. He is, however, courageous, determined, and extremely clever and resourceful, and most readers of the story and viewers of the film find him fascinating.

This is not to say that a hero can't be admirable or likable. In fact, it's often easier to get the reader involved in a story where the hero is admirable and likable, but it's not a required quality.

The Hero Has a "Special" Talent

A *special talent* is one of the qualities, Joseph Campbell points out, that endears the hero to the reader and convinces the reader that the hero's cause is just. This may not be completely true because a villain can have special talents as well, and we certainly don't want the reader convinced that the villain's cause is just. But the hero's special talent is an important factor in the reader's being able to identify with the hero and makes the hero more interesting as well. If I were to say to you, "It's uncanny, but my neighbor can flip a coin and tell you nine times of out ten if it'll be heads or tails," you would probably like to meet my neighbor.

You'd probably want to meet my neighbor if I told you she won the Betty Crocker bake-off last year, or she speaks twenty-seven languages, or she turned twelve thousand dollars into a hundred thousand in the futures market in a week. Special talents attract us. It's part of the human condition that we're fascinated by people who can do what others can't, be it untying the Gordian knot, teaching goldfish to go-go dance, or playing the banjo and the harmonica at the same time. A friend of mine can do that quite well, and though most people I know think it's a rather weird, backwoods sort of special talent, he seems to attract an audience wherever he goes.

The question usually arises about the relationship between the hero's special talent and his or her mission in the story. I'm often asked if the special talent needs to be the thing that brings the hero victory. Robin Hood's special talent, a phenomenal accuracy with a bow and arrow, certainly helps him in his struggle against the Sheriff of Nottingham and Prince John. Sherlock Holmes has special talents of deduction; so do Colombo, Miss Marple, Hercule Poirot, and Jessica Fletcher. All of these characters use their special talents in the course of their missions.

The strange thing is, the hero may have a special talent that isn't used in the course of his or her mission, but the special talent works its magic on the reader or viewer nevertheless.

The special talent makes the hero special. He or she is not an everyday person. The special talent sets the hero apart. James Bond, as an example, can taste a brandy and tell you what vineyard in France grew the grape and in what year. I don't know if that's actually possible; nonetheless it's an interesting trait. Speaking of what's not possible, I've often wondered if it is physically possible to split an arrow stuck in a target at a hundred yards. Robin Hood did it, and when I saw it in the film, I believed it. Of course I was only six years old at the time.

It doesn't matter if it's really possible in the real world. It is possible in the mythic world. The point is, the special talent impresses the reader or viewer and creates a bond between the reader or viewer and the hero, drawing the reader inexorably into the story. It proves that the hero is blessed by the gods.

A special talent might be a photographic memory, psychic powers, a talent for tossing horseshoe ringers, taming grizzlies, picking winners at the track, growing prize-winning flowers, working math problems, writing haiku—virtually anything that is exceptional.

Sometimes finding the special talent for the hero takes quite a bit of brainstorming, but it is usually well worth the effort. The special talent is the green chili on the taco.

The Hero Is an "Outlaw," Living by His or Her Own Rules

The hero is an outlaw in the sense that he or she plays by his or her own rules. Colombo is an outlaw. He doesn't drive the standard police car, he wears a rumpled trench coat, smokes cigars, and so on. Sherlock Holmes is not only a brilliant detective, he is a drug addict. McMurphy, in *One*

Flew over the Cuckoo's Nest, is certainly an outlaw, leading the rebellion against Big Nurse. How about Scrooge in *A Christmas Carol*—he's certainly at odds with society, living by his own rules. Humbert Humbert, in *Lolita,* is a child molester, a real outlaw. Michael Corleone, in *The Godfather,* is a professional gangster. Raskolnikov, in *Crime and Punishment,* is definitely an outlaw when he beans the old lady pawnbroker with an ax.

The hero need not be an extreme outlaw. It might be enough, as an example, that he turn away from the family law firm to work as a teamster. If the hero is not an outlaw, at least he or she is rebellious in some way.

Some mythologists have theories about the hero's being an outlaw because they claim the hero is taking society in directions in which society does not want to go. The hero is breaking new ground and therefore can't be a conformist.

An exception to this rule is found in the romance novel. In the romance novel, the protagonist is the heroine who falls in love with a "hero." In this case, the hero is almost always the outlaw, and the heroine, at the opening of the story, is more conventional. She's working on her Ph.D. in anthropology at Princeton; he's the leader of a motorcycle gang. Bammo! they fall in love, right off the bat. The outlaw hero is, of course, opposed by the heroine's family and friends and coworkers, but in the end, love triumphs and the heroine enters into a committed relationship with the outlaw hero. In a sense, she thus becomes an outlaw in the course of the story.

The Hero Is Good at What He or She Does for a Living

Say I were to tell you that my daughter's boyfriend works at a gas station. He comes in late, is rude to the customers, and can't make change very well. Would you want to know him? No. You'd think he was a jerk.

In all Western cultures most people are repulsed by those who don't do a good job. In America, where the work ethic—though perhaps a bit tarnished of late—is still strong, we're particularly repulsed by sloppy workmanship and discourteous or surly workers.

If I were to say that my daughter is dating a fellow who's a gas station attendant and just got the attendant-of-the-month award from his boss—always courteous, points out when customers' lights aren't working, offers to check the oil, etc.—you'd think highly of him. You'd think my daughter was dating a worthy person, despite the fact that being a gas station attendant is not generally considered a high-status job.

We respect people who are good at what they do for a living, and we disrespect people who are not. It's the same with fictional characters. We feel respect for characters who are good at what they do for a living, and we disrespect characters who are not.

A good example is Brody, the cop-hero in *Jaws* (1974). He's efficient, knows his men, and is way ahead of the rest of the town in perceiving the threat of the shark.

Scrooge, in *A Christmas Carol,* is certainly a great businessman, even though he's a total failure as a human being.

Humbert Humbert, in *Lolita*, is a degenerate, but he's good at what he does for a living—teaching literature.

Leamas, in *The Spy Who Came in from the Cold* (1963), is a master spy. We see from the very first that he's good at what he does.

The old man, in *The Old Man and the Sea*, is certainly good at what he does for a living, even though at the opening of the story he hasn't caught a fish in eighty-four days.

In *The Godfather*, Michael Corleone is a soldier at the opening of the story, just returned from fighting in World War II. He's a decorated war hero.

At the beginning of *Gone with the Wind*, Scarlett O'Hara is a Southern belle, whose job it is to attract a beau. The story starts: "Scarlett O'Hara was not beautiful, but men seldom realized it when caught by her charm." She's good at what she does. Later, of course, she becomes a terrific manager of her plantation and a dynamite businesswoman.

There are some exceptions to this, of course. The hero may, at the start of the story, be stuck in a horrible job that he or she does poorly. In this case, however, the reader or viewer can see that the hero is definitely not fit for this work and will soon have another occupation.

The Hero Is a Protagonist (Takes the Lead in a Cause or Action at Some Point in the Story)

The *protagonist* of a story is defined by *Webster's* as "one who takes the lead in a cause or action." Of course, the hero may not necessarily begin as the protagonist of the story, but at some point, he or she will take the lead. Scarlett O'Hara,

as an example, does not take the lead at first. She's content
to sit out the war. She wants it over so she can go back to
the sort of life she loves—being a Southern belle. But after
Tara, her family's plantation, is wrecked, she becomes a protagonist.

Henry, the protagonist of *The Red Badge of Courage,* at
first runs from the enemy, but later finds his courage and
becomes a protagonist.

Michael Corleone, in *The Godfather,* at first rejects the
family business, but when his father is shot, Michael becomes a protagonist. He kills two of his father's enemies.

The hero must be a protagonist. If he is not, the character
who is a protagonist is the central character, the focus of the
story.

Mitch McDeere, in *The Firm,* does not become a protagonist at first—he goes along with the firm. Only when he
wakes up to their illegal activity does he spring to action.

The Hero Has Been "Wounded" (Maimed, Disgraced, Grieving for a Lost Loved One, Etc.) or Is Wounded in the Course of the Story

The hero's wound is an extremely important aspect of the
hero's makeup. The wound makes the hero human. The
wound draws the reader's sympathy. The wound makes the
hero's life in some sense pathos, even tragedy. The wound
gives the hero the need to be healed, usually by love or right-
ing a wrong.

The wound can be physical, psychological, spiritual, social—anything that causes the hero to suffer. The hero may
have been disgraced in the past—perhaps he or she has been

fired from a job unjustly or unjustly convicted of a crime. He or she may have lost a lover to death or to a rival, may have been shot, beaten, robbed, or humiliated. The wound may even be, in some sense, self-inflicted. The hero may have given in to temptation, may be a drunk or a drug addict, or the like. And the deeper, the more painful, the better.

Scrooge is wounded by his terrible childhood. Brody, in *Jaws*, is wounded by his wife's infidelity. Leamas is wounded by his Cold War weariness; Henry, in *The Red Badge of Courage*, by his guilt. Scarlett is wounded by the loss of her way of life. The old man, in *The Old Man and the Sea*, is wounded by the humiliation of going eighty-four days without catching a fish.

It may be unpleasant, especially if you love your hero, but it must be done. Heroes need to suffer.

The Hero Is Motivated by Idealism—at Least at Some Point in the Story

Idealism here has a broad interpretation. The hero need not be philosophically committed to a cause, nor be an idealist in the usual sense of the word. Here, idealism is used in the sense of altruism, the opposite of egoism. The hero—at least in some part of the story—is not motivated by selfish reasons but sacrifices himself for the good of others.

Often, at the beginning of a story, the hero is not self-sacrificing but is interested only in self. This loss of selfishness is one of the strongest motifs in myth-based fiction. McMurphy, the sociopath, works for the good of the other patients, trying to get them to rebel against the tyranny of Big Nurse. Scrooge, in the end, becomes the Santa Claus, bringing the spirit of Christmas all year round to everyone he meets. Henry goes into battle for his country. Scarlett O'Hara sacrifices for her community, her plantation, when she rebuilds Tara. Brody risks his life for his community when he goes out to fight the shark.

The Hero Is Sexually Potent

Sex sells, it is said in the ad game. The largest genre (in terms of numbers of books sold) by far in the publishing industry is the romance novel. Sexual tension turns up the voltage of your story.

It's difficult for a reader to identify with a eunuch.

There are some well-known novels that are exceptions to this, such as Anne Rice's *Cry to Heaven* (1982), about singing castrati, or Hemingway's *The Sun Also Rises* (1926) with Jake Barnes. These are both moving stories, but the effect is not one of dramatic character transformation on the hero's journey. Rather, they evoke pity and ennui and are interesting character studies that the reader watches with fascination, perhaps, but does not fully participate in because he or she cannot identify with them. You take a great risk when you make your hero sexually impotent in any novel, myth based or not. Creating a mythic character without sexual energy is like bringing the burgers, the buns, and the charcoal to the barbecue, and leaving the matches at home.

Other Qualities of the Hero

In addition to the qualities the hero always possesses, discussed above, there are other qualities that the hero may or may not possess:

The Hero Very Often Has Hubris (a Big Head)

This is an extremely common trait. Think of Samson, McMurphy, Scrooge, Scarlett O'Hara, Humbert Humbert—big heads all.

The Hero Is Usually Stoical

The stoical hero has a long tradition. The hero usually accepts pain and suffering without complaint and is sometimes extremely stoical, enduring torture without flinching. The hero sometimes endures not only great physical pain, but tremendous emotional pain as well.

The Hero Is Usually Loyal

Loyalty is very common in the hero. As an example, Scarlett O'Hara is loyal to Tara; in fact, her loyalty is at the center of the work. Robin Hood is loyal to the men of Sherwood. Michael Corleone is loyal to his family.

The Hero Is Usually Considered Sexually Appealing

Robin Hood again, Michael Corleone, McMurphy, Scarlett O'Hara . . . almost all heroes are sexually appealing. Scrooge, of course, would be an exception.

The Hero Is Sometimes Physically Superior in Some Way (Strength, Speed, Hearing, Reflexes, Etc.)

James Bond can fight like ten tigers. Robin Hood has exceptional eye-hand coordination. Hercules was a great wrestler. If you count IQ as a physical trait, you can include Sherlock Holmes, Miss Marple, and Colombo as examples.

The Hero Sometimes Has a Special Birth (a Parent Might Be a King, a Doomed Prisoner, a Goddess, an Apache Warrior, and the Like)

The old myths were full of such things. Scarlett O'Hara's special pedigree is spelled out in the first few sentences of *Gone With the Wind*. She had the "delicate features of her mother, a Coast aristocrat of French descent. . . ."

The Hero Sometimes Has a Special Destiny (Predicted by a Seer, Perhaps)

Macbeth has such a destiny, as spelled out by the three witches.

The Hero Is Sometimes Branded—Has a Special Mark, Scar, Tattoo, or the Like

This is often a birthmark, proving the hero is a king or duke or something. Samson's hair, a symbol of his dedication to God, is such a symbol.

The Hero Is Sometimes Cynical

The cynical hero has a long tradition in American popular fiction. Authors from Raymond Chandler and Dashiel Hammet to Elmore Leonard and Sara Paretski use the cynical hero to great effect. The cynicism usually comes from a jaded idealism. The hero is wounded, suffering stoically; the cynicism is a balm for the hero's wounds. Scrooge is an extreme example.

The Hero Is Sometimes "Mouthy": Known as a "Wise Guy," If a Man; "Sharp-Tongued," If a Woman

The hero, being a cynic, usually can't keep quiet, and therefore is known as "mouthy" or "sharp-tongued." McMurphy, in *One Flew over the Cuckoo's Nest*, is an example. Most detectives are mouthy cynics, jaded as a New York streetwalker.

Okay, we now have an inventory of the hero's traits. You may have read that a hero needs a *flaw*. Aristotle said in *The Poetics* that the tragic hero needs a flaw or lack—say, he lacks compassion. Flaw or lack, it doesn't really matter. Aristotle was speaking of the special case of the tragic hero, which will be discussed in chapter 9. The standard hero may have a such a flaw or may not. It's not required. If the hero has a wound, it's enough. He or she will need to be healed.

In the next chapter we get on with the creation of a particular hero who will embody the heroic traits—who will then be paired and contrasted with the Evil One.

3

The Twin Pillars of the Myth-Based Story: The Hero and the Evil One

Characters Not of Wood

The importance of creating interesting, three-dimensional, well-rounded characters for your myth-based story cannot be overstressed. Creating a myth-based modern story is not simply a matter of tossing in mythic elements as they do in cheap rip-offs of mythic stories on TV and in many action-adventure movies and novels. Creating the modern myth-based story requires forming it from the ground up, which means that the characters (the foundation for all good fiction) need to be real, flesh-and-blood, fully rounded, good, dramatic characters—in addition to possessing mythic qualities.

Often today in fiction and films we find heroes who are cartoonish cutouts, invulnerable supermen who can leap over tall buildings with a single bound. Such heroes are the Supermen, the Batmen, the Spidermen; the Rambos, the James Bonds, and the Indiana Joneses. Among the female incarnations of the cartoon hero are Wonder Woman and Xena,

Warrior Princess, a character who is currently achieving astounding TV ratings. The charm of cartoon heroes is that they fight for justice and can crush their enemies, and we can all identify with that. Such characters are sometimes immensely entertaining and can be as much fun as a two-hour Road Runner cartoon; however, they lack the ability to profoundly move the reader. The stories about these characters may conform to the monomyth in a superficial way, but because these heroes often lack a wound and have no weakness or vulnerability, they are not fully human. In fact, they cannot be wounded deeply because they're emotionally armor plated. Such characters go through the motions, but they have no potential for transformation inside, which is at the heart of a deeply satisfying, myth-based story.

When creating a character for a myth-based story, all the principles and techniques of craft discussed in *How to Write a Damn Good Novel* and *How to Write a Damn Good Novel II: Advanced Techniques* still apply. The hero needs to have three dimensions: physiological, sociological, and psychological. The hero needs to be interesting to the reader, an extreme example of type, dramatically driven, have a ruling passion, and so on.

It's all well and good to talk about the characteristic traits of the hero and to say that the hero needs to be vulnerable and a flesh-and-blood character, and so on, but just how does one go about creating such characters, and how does one go about creating a hero's journey? Where to begin?

You start by dreaming up a heroic character, using the brainstorming technique discussed in *How to Write a Damn Good Novel*; you create him/her with three dimensions, a sociology, a physiology, and a psychology; and you make sure that you include the heroic qualities discussed in the last chapter.

Because in the *How to Write a Damn Good Novel* books I created stories with male protagonists, I'll create a female hero for an example of a mythic hero in *The Blue Light*. The hero's journey is often depicted as a male thing, which it definitely is not. Perhaps, in antiquity, most of the myths did have male heroes. But not all. It's been estimated by some mythologist with a lot of grant money to blow on research assistants that about 85 percent of the world's myths feature male heroes and 15 percent feature female heroes. The form of the monomyth remains unchanged, however. There are a few small differences with the female hero in the way she may approach the solution to a problem, the way she may seek counsel from the Wise One, the way she might deal with aggression, but these are simply the differences between men and women that would apply even if the story were not myth based.

Creating the Hero for *The Blue Light*

Okay, so the place to start creating a hero is with a name. Hummmmmm . . . let's see, Nancy, Beth, Jane, Rae, Sam, Mindy, Ulma, Frances, Candy, Sandra. . . .

How about "Sandra Holland"?

Okay? I'm not sold on the name, I'm just trying it out. Names are critically important and require some thought. Change the name, and you change the reader's perception of the character. A psychologist made a study of names and found that women with, let us say, "coarse" names such as

"Olga" and "Bertha" reported twice as much depression as women with less coarse names like "Heidi" and "Candy Sue." Of course, Candy Sue might want to change her name if she's applying to medical school. You see, it does make a difference. Would you like your brain surgeon to be called "Yum Yum Butterfly"?

A name says a lot about a person. Often, people who don't like their names go by a nickname. Stanley Smigelski might be known as "Butcher" Smigelski if he's in Al Capone's gang or "The Polish Nightingale" if he's a cabaret crooner.

Readers take characters' names to be clues to their personalities. The name "Olga Kurtzkoff" and the name "Penny Wonderbee" strike the reader quite differently. It's difficult to imagine Olga as a petite blonde with dimples, or Penny as a haggard old bag.

So how about Sandra Holland?

Naomi Holland?

Linda Holland?

Pat Holland?

We could go on. The one that suits me is "Naomi." It's unusual, yet not bizarre. Let's go with "Naomi Garret Holland," at least for the moment. Let's say "Garret" was her mother's maiden name. Let's say she prefers to be called Garret rather than Naomi.

Garret Holland.

Okay, we have our hero's name. Now, let's start describing her in terms of her physiology, sociology, and psychology, following the instructions for creating characters from scratch.

Our Hero's Physiology

As an adult, Garret is five-five and 120 with a firm body. Lithe and agile, she dances and works out often. She has her dishwater blonde hair cut in a short bob so it will be easy to take care of. Let's give her ice blue eyes. I like ice blue eyes.

Garret has a pretty face with a straight nose and a small mouth with perfect teeth. Her hands and wrists are delicate, and she carries tennis balls to squeeze to build her strength. She detests weakness. She has a high IQ. From her earliest years she's had a ringing in her ears that comes and goes. Sometimes she can almost hear a voice in the ringing, but can never make out the words.

There's a white spot on the top of her right breast where she had a tattoo of a tiger removed. She got the tattoo while in college when out with her sorority sisters for a night on the town, and her mother had her remove it as soon as she found out. Garret's motor has always seemed to be revved up. She does everything fast. She's a perpetual whirlwind, always on the move.

Our Hero's Sociology

Where was Garret born? Let's say New York City. Let's say her father was Kirk Holland, a legendary political reporter for the *New York Herald Tribune,* and her mother's father was Lloyd Garret, publisher of the *New York Post.* Garret was born with newspaper ink in her veins.

Her mother was a socialite, and the family lived on New York's Upper West Side. Garret's parents divorced when she was four, and she lived with her mother, a social butterfly whom she rarely saw. She visited her father every Sunday, and they spent most of their time together at the newspaper office. Her father's passion for newspapers became her passion.

Growing up, she went to summer camp and sailed in racing boats on Long Island Sound. She loves the water. Her mother never seemed to have time for her, and her father was always working. But her father did help her on her stories, and it was the one thing that linked them together. She was brought up by servants, mainly an African-American maid by the name of Sarah Washington, a jovial, pipe-smoking, affectionate woman, the only person Garret felt truly loved her. Garret called her "Aunt Sarah."

Garret's moving obituary of Sarah Washington, when she died of a stroke at sixty-seven, titled "Just a Maid," won Garret a "first-person writing" award at Yale. When she started at the paper where she works now, it was reprinted as a character piece in the paper's Sunday supplement.

Garret worked on a newspaper in high school and at Yale, and when she graduated at twenty, she went to work for the *New York Post*, the youngest reporter they'd hired in twenty years. Beyond just being a good reporter, she became a champion dart thrower. The gang from work hung out in an English pub–style bar that featured darts. She couldn't stand losing, so she took lessons, set up a dartboard in her home, and became an expert.

Her father died of a massive stroke the same year she started her career at the *New York Post*.

Garret was always ambitious, studious, focused, hard-driving. In college she fell madly in love with a quarterback who loved her too, until he met her roommate (and best friend), whose father owned Wall Street's biggest brokerage firm. The split-up crushed Garret, and she never got over the sense of double betrayal. Now she has no time in her life for serious relationships with men. She enjoys sex, but she doesn't like attachment, she tells herself—attachment means giving one's time, and she has no time to give. She sees marriage as a cage she wants desperately to stay out of. As soon as a man she's dating sounds serious, she breaks up with him.

One of the men she broke up with was an assistant DA who knew about her amphetamine habit. She'd become addicted while in college. She used the pills to diet and to stay up late to study. They needed a high-profile drug case, and she was elected. "*New York Post* Reporter Jailed in Drug Bust," the headlines read. She was fired. Disgraced, she went to work in the only place she could find a job—Reno, Nevada—for a third of what she had been making in New York. It's not the money, it's the feeling of being exiled that gets her. Being in Nowheresville, Siberia.

She quit drugs cold turkey. She would never go to a twelve-step program; she'd never admit to a weakness in public like that.

Our Hero's Psychology

Now in her late twenties, Garret is a workaholic. Ambitious, smart, driven, talented, and cocksure of herself. As a reporter, she knows she's gifted. What makes her special is that she will do anything to get a story and she can write it at lightning speed. But the approval she always wanted from Dad never quite got there. No article she ever did was quite good enough. He was a perfectionist. He's been dead now for eight years, and it seems he's still looking over her shoulder, driving her on with a whip.

Now that she's been fired and exiled to a hellhole like Reno (in her view; I'm actually fond of the place), she has but one ambition—to score a story that will get her back to the Big City. This is her ruling passion. To get that big story she will do . . . whatever it takes.

She believes that journalism is entertainment. She thinks that journalists cannot expose official corruption or keep the public informed on vital issues if first the news is not entertaining—the public has too many other entertainment choices competing against the news. She sees news as drama, and she's a playwright; the people in the news are her characters.

In her personal life she stays clear of serious relationships.

It's important to find the voice of the character and to get into the character's head. One way to do this (as discussed in *How to Write a Damn Good Novel*) is to "interview" the character. Another method is to write a journal in the character's voice. The idea is to just let your imagination go and try to feel what it's like to be Garret.

Garret's Journal, Written in Her Voice

Okay, so here I sit on my tush in goddamn Reno—billed as the Biggest Little City on Earth—writing stories about the opening of the Grand Deuces Casino and the dog show at the Hilton, and manning the rewrite desk every damn Friday. Today I E-mailed a letter to Eddie Jackson at the *Washington Post* begging for a job, and he E-mailed me back saying even God didn't have that much pull. The newspaper business is a small club.

I'm going mad.

Last night I went back to the Lucky Duck and lost a hundred bucks playing roulette and waited for Jerry to get off work and had too many tequila sunrises at the bar. We had a prime rib dinner at Harrahs, then went over to his place and massaged each other and played other games until three in the morning. Jerry's an okay guy, but the biggest thing in his life seems to be being a shift manager of a two-bit casino, and he loves this Biggest Little Dump on Earth.

Last month I was assigned to do a personality profile of a hooker at the legal brothel just out of town called "Bo Honey's Ranch." She had the morals of a Dumpster and the brains of an oyster. The paper wanted her portrayed as a hero of women's liberation, and that's what I gave them. I'm here to please, anything, just so long as I can get the hell out of here.

I'm going stark-raving mad.

Last week they had me covering the Western States Bowling Tournament. Reno is the damn bowling capital of the world. Five hundred lanes at the tournament center built at the taxpayers' expense.

Bowling pins have bounced around in my head every night since. The big story was that a guy bowled a 299 game—missed a perfect game by one pin. He lay on the alley pounding his feet and fists like a spoiled kid denied an ice-cream cone.

Lenny Fargo, the assistant editor, said to me last night that I should keep up the good work and he'll let me be the vacation relief covering the city council. Fred Hill has been covering the city council for twenty-three years and still has twelve years to go to retirement. Around here that's considered a plumb assignment. There's nothing quite so scintillating as watching a dozen gray-hairs debating the virtues of new benches in Truckee Park.

Really, I am going mad.

The lead story this morning had to do with fifty cows that got loose on Highway 12 and stopped traffic going to Tahoe for six hours.

I remember how it was back in New York, covering the UN. Covering the murder of Madam Reneaux, covering the trial of the Bronx Eleven, covering the crime commission hearings on police corruption. Every day was exciting; every day something new was happening.

There I worked with people who felt passionately about their work, people who thought what they were doing meant something. Now I'm bleeding my life away a drop at a time, writing drivel about cows tying up the goddamn traffic. . . . Hey, and by the way, Mr. Author, I'm not in love with the name you picked out for me. Naomi. Too many vowels. You're right, I prefer to go by my middle name, Garret. Seems to me it has an edge to it, and I'm definitely on edge.

And you say you wanted me to talk about how I felt about my father and mother. Mom was as cold as iced mackerel. Dad was warmer, a workaholic, brilliant, with a great sense of humor, the best. He always pushed me hard, the way I should have been pushed.

I loved my father deeply, and I think, well. . . . I think he was fond of me, but neither of my parents was really capable of love.

God, I hate to talk about this. Only the maid, Sarah, really cared about me, if you want to know the truth.

About my love life. Hey, I loved once. I was young and stupid; I toppled easily. I melted every time he turned his gaze toward me. The best thing that ever happened to me was his going south. He wasn't really my type. Who is? Nobody. I agree with Gloria Steinem's great quote, "A woman needs a man like a fish needs a bicycle. . . ."

This journal, of course, would go on for several more pages—this short section is only a sample. This is the part of fiction writing that's fun. No one is ever going to see these journals—they are for the writer's benefit. In the classes I've taught I've found that this method of first-person journal writing is the best way for writers to get into the heads of their characters. It's similar to what "method" actors do to get into character. Let your imagination run riot.

So, then, how is Garret as a suitable dramatic character?

In *How to Write a Damn Good Novel, II* there's a section

in chapter 3 on making characters interesting—in addition to making them good dramatic characters. I wrote that what made characters dynamic was that they had "strong emotions . . . the inner emotional fires are raging." In addition, they should be interesting; they should have been to interesting places and done interesting things; and they should have a philosophy, you might say, and a fresh attitude toward life, an individual angle. I believe Garret is such a character.

But is she a suitable hero for a myth-based story?

Because she's not Xena, Warrior Princess, you might think she's not suitable. The modern mythic hero is not a warrior prince or princess; modern mythic heroes are flesh-and-blood, real human beings who possess heroic qualities.

Let's see, heroes are outlaws, living by their own rules. Well, in one sense Garret's an outlaw—she was addicted to amphetamines—and we'll see that she does things in very unorthodox ways. She's certainly good at what she does for a living and has a lot of hubris. She has special talents: she's a great journalist, as we'll observe when she gets into action, and she's a great dart thrower. She's definitely a protagonist. She's been deeply wounded. She's motivated by idealism: she wants to get people to read newspapers. She's sexually potent and sexually appealing. She's loyal to her profession and has a superior ability to write stories. She has a special birth: her mother was from high society and her father, a newspaper legend. She has always felt—and was told by her father all her young life—that she was destined to be a great reporter, which only goes to heighten her wound. We'll see later, when she's trapped in the desert, that she's stoical, cynical, and no doubt sharp-tongued.

And, perhaps most important, Garret has the potential

for transformation. Her wounds—her soul-poisoning anger at being kicked out of the big time and being dumped by the only man she ever loved—may heal in the course of the story. The wall that separates her emotionally from real love may be knocked down. Although she has the major mythic qualities—a special talent, a wound, being good at what she does—please note that she is not a superwoman. She's hurting and she's vulnerable, so she's both good hero material and completely human.

This sketch of Garret is a shortened version of what I'd do if I were actually writing a novel because I don't want to bore my readers with a lot of tedious detail. I've created Garret for demonstration purposes, to show how a heroic character is conceived. This kind of background material should fill many pages in preparation for writing an actual novel. Such sketches and journals are valuable aids for the writer in building good characters and getting to know them well. You don't have to worry about your grammar when you write them.

Spending the time to do extensive biographies and journals for your characters will help greatly when you begin drafting your story. Your characters will come alive on the page right from the start. I've discovered in working with hundreds of beginning writers that this method is extremely helpful.

What would a character be like who lacks heroic qualities? Some fiction touted as "literary" often features protagonists who are not heroes: Bloom in James Joyce's *Ulysses* (1922) is an example. Bloom, the central character, is pitifully unheroic. He's not even a decent protagonist. A protagonist is *a character who takes the lead in a cause or action.* Bloom just . . . well, he's just Bloom, bumbling through a day in Dublin in 1904, not doing much. He knows his wife is having an affair, yet he does nothing but moan and whine about it. *Ulysses* is supposed to be an echo of Homer's great heroic epic *The Odyssey*—in reality, it is only a pale shadow. It is not a tale of courageous, heroic action, but a finely written description of daily life's minutia in all its boring, banal details.

Virginia Woolf's Mrs. Dalloway of *Mrs. Dalloway* (1925) is not a hero. Again, we have a character in a single day thinking, remembering, but not taking any action, heroic or otherwise.

Antiheroic writing continues in American academic literature today.

In Richard Ford's successful, finely written, and well-reviewed *The Sportswriter* (1986), main character Frank Bascombe, a latter-day Bloom, is not a hero. He takes no heroic action. The book is about a man who regrets having given up a literary career to become a sportswriter and how he comes to terms with it. Much so-called literary fiction is rife with stories and antistories involving antiheroes, villains-as-protagonists, and slice-of-life pieces that have no heroes and often no protagonists. Some works of literature are simply fictional essays, poetic or philosophical pieces; the delight in reading them is the observation of life and the music of the fine writing. True, in literary fiction the prose is often poetic, the metaphors are often fresh and snappy, and the dialogue sparkles. And almost always these works are deadly boring because they don't have the power to make the reader dream the fictive dream and they have no drama, no moral choices, to test the characters and probe the characters' depths.

The Role of the Evil One and the Art of Being Pivotal

Now that we have the hero, the next most important character is that of the Evil One, even though the Evil One may not be on stage in front of the reader. In some stories the Evil One is often on stage; in others, not. The role of the Evil One is to hatch an evil plot and to carry it out. The Evil One usually provides most of the tests and trials of the hero.

Not only does the Evil One put obstacles in the hero's path, but the Evil One is also an evil presence that creates a sense of menace. Myth-based fictional works, at their core, are stories in which the self-sacrificing hero is at war with the selfish, self-centered Evil One.

Though the Evil One is usually the hero's chief antagonist, there are cases when the Evil One's henchmen present more of an immediate and dire threat to the hero. *The African Queen* is a good example. The Evil One is Kaiser Wilhelm of Germany, who's not even a character in the story. His henchmen are the two heroes' chief antagonists. The Kaiser does, however, cast a pall of menace and doom.

The Evil One hatches what we can call the "plot behind the plot." In a murder mystery, as an example, the plot behind the plot is the murderous plan of the Evil One to commit the murder and his or her attempts to escape from justice.

Lajos Egri, in *The Art of Dramatic Writing*, called certain characters "pivotal." The Evil One is such a character. A pivotal character "pushes the action." Egri uses Iago, the villain in Shakespeare's *Othello*, as one example. Iago has it in for Othello. He fills the easily dupable Othello's ears with all sorts of lies about Desdemona, Othello's lovely and faithful wife. It's a long, sad story, but, in brief, Othello listens to the Evil One and ends up stabbing poor Desdemona to death. Iago is pivotal—he pushes the action. Without him, Othello would never take action. When Othello does commit to the deed, he becomes pivotal. And yes, you can have two or more characters being pivotal at the same time. Both sides in a battle may be taking action, as an example. In a South American soccer match, both teams may be pivotal, and so might all the rioters in the stands.

When creating any kind of dramatic fiction, you need to have some character pushing the action. Of course, the pivotal character can change: in a detective story, for instance, the murderer (the Evil One) is pivotal when committing the murder and may simply hole up thereafter and stop pushing the action, at which point some other character, usually the detective, will start pushing the action. When no character pushes the action, a story loses its momentum. Think of pivotal characters as your story's propulsion system—they provide the torque.

Normally it is the Evil One who necessitates the call to adventure that will cause the hero to leave the world of the everyday. The Evil One is, in one sense, the author of the story.

Since it is the Evil One who will be pushing the action, let's get on with creating one for *The Blue Light*.

Creating the Evil One

In creating the Evil One, you should keep the following qualities in mind. Some of them are shared with the hero; some are not.

Like the Hero, the Evil One May Be Full of Hubris

Both the hero and the Evil One may think of themselves as the greatest. James Bond and Goldfinger, as an example, both have egos the size of Montana. So do Sherlock Holmes and Moriarty and McMurphy and Big Nurse. The list is endless.

Like the Hero, the Evil One May Be an Outlaw

The Evil One, however, is not an outlaw in the same sense that the hero is. The hero usually just defies conventionality, by smoking cigars at the church picnic, as an example. He or she may even be a more extreme outlaw—a rogue or a highwayman—but never a vicious criminal. The Evil One, of course, is often a vicious criminal. But more often than not, the Evil One is not publicly an outlaw, at least in the eyes of the law and society. Big Nurse, as far as society is concerned, is an excellent and effective nurse, running a nice clean ward, taking care of her patients in an exemplary manner. The mayor in *Jaws* is an upstanding citizen as well. He risks lives so he and the rest of the upstanding citizens of the town can make a buck during the tourist season.

Like the Hero, the Evil One Is Clever and Resourceful

If the Evil One is not clever and resourceful, even more clever and resourceful at times than the hero, the story is apt to be a dull one. Interesting stories come from the machinations of two worthy opponents. If the Evil One is easily defeated because of ineptitude or stupidity, the story will be flat or unintentionally comic.

Like the Hero, the Evil One May Be Wounded

That the Evil One may be wounded sounds a little contradictory, since the point of the hero's wound is to gain sympathy for the hero. The Evil One's wound might gain sympathy for the Evil One, were it not for the fact that often he or she uses the wound as an excuse for doing evil. The reader or viewer does not feel sorry for Dr. No because he has lost his hands.

Like the Hero, the Evil One May Have a Special Talent

The Evil One's special talent is somewhat problematical. Joseph Campbell observed that the special talent is a quality of the hero that puts us on the hero's side and makes his or her cause our cause. But this is not the case for the Evil One. Why? Usually, the Evil One's special talent is used for evil. If the hero and the Evil One both have the same skill—say they're both great swordsmen—the usual pattern is that the Evil One wins most of the contests but loses the last. The hero's talents usually improve, while the Evil One becomes more overconfident or more frustrated.

Like the Hero, the Evil One May Have Great Sex Appeal

The sex appeal of the Evil One is pretty much a Hollywood cliché. It's a cliché because it always wins over audiences. That evil has its attractions is as old a theme as myth itself. Ulysses found Circe, the evil witch, beautiful, alluring, and sexy.

The following qualities are not shared by the hero and the Evil One.

Unlike the Hero, the Evil One Is Motivated by Greed, Avarice, Lust, Lust for Power, Vanity, Narcissism, and So On

The hero may have such motives in the beginning of the story, but will abandon such self-serving motives later on. But not the Evil One. The Evil One is always out for himself. What the Evil One wants is to satisfy his own ego and that's it. There are some Freudian psychologists who theorize that heroic literature is actually a reflection of the human psyche and the war between the id and the ego and superego. In other words, they see heroic literature as a metaphor for the struggle between the base animal nature buried deep in the psyche of us all and our reason and conscience. Or, you might say, between the "inner child" and the "inner adult." The Evil One, then, is a metaphor for the id—the inner child. The Evil One is like a greedy, spoiled adolescent wholly concerned with Me-Me-Me. The hero is an adult, concerned with sacrificing himself for others and bringing a boon to the community.

Often in cartoon-type myth-based stories, the James Bond/Indiana Jones type, the greed of the Evil One is titanic. Goldfinger wanted, I guess, all the gold on earth. Dr. No wanted to rule the universe. Sherlock Holmes's Evil One, Moriarty, wanted to be the most fiendish criminal genius in history. Now there was a great Evil One. In the less cartoonish type of myth-based fiction, the Evil Ones have more subtlety. Their motives are perhaps just as base, but they don't sneer, cackle, and posture quite so much.

Unlike the Hero, the Evil One Never Acts Out of Idealism

The Evil One isn't idealistic—at least he or she has no ideal a sane person would think of as being idealistic. The Evil One does not at any time operate for the good of others unless they are his or her own family, which is just another kind of vanity and selfishness. The Evil One is fully committed to enriching the Evil One. Where the hero will, at least in some part of the story, act for the good of others, the Evil One is out for himself or herself from beginning to end. If the Evil One appears to be operating out of idealism, it is a self-serving idealism.

Unlike the Hero, the Evil One Is Often Cruel

The Evil One's cruelty is another quality that is often emphasized in cartoon-type myth-based stories. In *One Flew over the Cuckoo's Nest*, Big Nurse is cruel. Deliciously so. In *Carrie*, Carrie's mother is the Evil One (at least one of the Evil Ones); she's just as cruel as Big Nurse, though she wraps herself in the Bible. In *The Firm*, the Mafia boss who's actually running the firm is certainly cruel. In the 1950s film *A Christmas Carol*, the Evil One is Scrooge's father, who treats young Ebenezer horribly, punishing him because he lived when his mother died giving birth to him. In some stories, the cruelty is overblown to the point of absurdity, such as in the Batman films and TV show. The Joker and the Riddler are portraits of pure malice, with all the posturing, boasting, and cackling that goes with caricatured evil.

Unlike the Hero, the Evil One May Win by Luck

The Evil One often is quite lucky in the beginning and middle of a story. There is in every story an "obligatory scene." It is not often talked about by dramatic theorists because it is a natural consequence of the design of a dramatic story. The obligatory scene is the scene in which the main story question, the central story question, which is a product of the core conflict, is answered. As an example, in a romance it is the moment when both lovers acknowledge they're meant for each other. In a mystery, it is the moment the detective figures out who the killer is. After the obligatory scene, there follow the actions that stem from it. In the romance, the lovers are bonded together. In the mystery, the detective traps the killer. It's common for luck to be on the side of the Evil One until the obligatory scene and on the side of the hero thereafter. The reason for this, I believe, is that once the murderer is identified and all that's left is the climax, the reader is impatient with more complications and wants the actions to settle the matter—wants the lovers to get married, the killer caught, or whatever. Sometimes there is no separate obligatory scene; it is incorporated into the climactic scene, or it happens out of view of the reader. In murder mysteries, this might happen when the detective, say, walks the floor all night figuring the case out and the next morning has a plan to trap the killer.

Unlike the Hero, the Evil One Is Not Forgiving

Forgiving is just not something evil people do. The Evil One may forgive a small thing, but not anything large. The Evil One, the narcissistic child, does not have a forgiving nature.

Unlike the Hero, the Evil One Might Quit—but Only at the Very End

The hero will never quit (except, possibly, very briefly during a moment of discouragement), but the Evil One may quit and run as the confrontation with the hero draws near. Think of Goldfinger abandoning his followers once the trap is sprung on him at Fort Knox. This sometimes shows an inherent cowardliness in the Evil One, which he or she will explain away as "the better part of valor" or some such drivel.

Though it is true that the Evil One may be courageous, more often than not the Evil One's show of courage is nothing more than posturing or bravado.

Unlike the Hero, the Evil One May Whine and Grovel

Evil ones don't always whine and grovel, but they've been known to do it. In *Othello,* once Iago is exposed as the villain, he whines and begs for his life. A hero would never do that.

Unlike the Hero, the Evil One May Not Be Stoical

Evil Ones are self-indulgent and therefore are hard put to put up with hardship. They often complain as well as whine.

Unlike the Hero, the Evil One May Not Be Loyal

The Evil One often turns on his friends and followers. In Shakespeare's *Macbeth* (1606), Macbeth has his friend Banquo killed, as an example.

Unlike the Hero, the Evil One Is Usually Not Physically Superior—Though His or Her Sidekick May Be

Big Nurse does not wrestle with the patients; she has aides to do that for her. Often when physical derring-do needs to be done, the Evil One will send out his or her minions to do it. In James Bond novels, Bloufelt sits and pets his cat and sends his lieutenants to do his dirty work.

Unlike the Hero, the Evil One Has No Special Birth or Special Destiny, Though He or She May Falsely Claim One

This is not to say that the Evil One may not be a prince or a king. Very often the Evil One is of the upper class and may have a title. But he is not born the night of the comet that spells his name out in the vapor trail. Only heroes have that sort of privilege.

The Case of the "Innocent" Evil One

Occasionally you may see a film or read a story in which the author lets the Evil One off the hook.

In the end, we find out that the Evil One didn't mean to do it, that he or she killed, say, by accident, and the story is about how he or she tried to cover it up. This is done when authors feel sorry for their own creation. Authors who do this often say, "Well, I wanted to make the Evil One human." While it's true that you'll want to create an Evil One in your story who is a human being, including writing the Evil One's full biography, you do not want your Evil One to commit bad acts by accident or out of good motives.

Nope, the Evil One needs to be evil, motivated by his own inner, selfish needs, and should never be self-sacrificing. Not if you're attempting to write a myth-based story. The myth-based story requires the Evil One to be evil. The reason for this is simple enough. One of the great satisfactions the reader gets from reading a myth-based story is the feeling that the hero, acting unselfishly for others, has confronted the Evil One, who is ruthlessly, consciously, willfully acting upon his or her own selfish interests. This does not mean that the hero need be victorious, though he or she usually is. The point is that, at a very deep level, the reader of a story or the viewer of a film is greatly moved by the nobility of the attempt on the part of the hero to defeat the Evil One. To discover in the end that the Evil One is not actually evil and is really something of a hero in disguise is a terrible letdown for the reader or viewer.

An exception is when the Evil One is serving some other ruling group, such as the Nazis. The Evil One may be self-sacrificing for an evil cause; that makes him just as evil in the reader's mind, however, as a selfish Evil One.

Creating the Evil One for *The Blue Light*

After brainstorming a bit, I came up with the Evil One for *The Blue Light*.

He's Morgan Thorn, the owner of a shoddy little casino on the outskirts of Reno, The Monkey's Paw. He also has a gold mine out in the desert, which happens to be near where the blue light is appearing in the sky.

Normally a coincidence, especially a huge coincidence like having the blue light and the mine just happen to be near each other, would be a violation of the rules of good dramatic fiction. But a coincidence at the beginning of a story, if it's the event that precipitates the initial actions of the story, is perfectly okay. Some other coincidences, if they favor the Evil One or his or her minions, may be okay as well later on.

To mine his gold, Morgan Thorn is using Mexicans

smuggled in to work for low wages. He's using no environmental protection whatever and keeping the mine completely hidden. The Evil One is doing evil indeed.

Naturally, such an important character will require a full biographical workup just as much as the hero.

When thinking of your Evil One, the important thing to remember is that unless you're writing a cartoon like James Bond or Indiana Jones, the Evil One should be a rounded character like any other and will have a physiology, a sociology, and a psychology.

Now then, what about Morgan Thorn?

The Evil One's Physiology

Morgan Thorn, at the time of the story, is sixty-three years old. He works out religiously and has a wonderful physique—"the body of a twenty-five year old," he is fond of saying. He's still handsome, with sandy brown hair, just now beginning to gray, and a square face and pale green eyes. His hair is receding, and he's constantly seeking treatments that promise to hold back the tide. He has a cunning intelligence and a quick temper.

The Evil One's Sociology

Morgan's father had come west as a young man. His father was a Thorn of the Boston Thorns, a socially prominent family in shipbuilding. Morgan's father had gotten a girl "in trouble," and, when he refused to marry her, she hung herself. Disgraced, Morgan's father came west and settled in Reno, where a friend he'd known while they were students at Harvard was a judge.

Morgan's father got into ranching and operated a local delivery trucking business. In business he was a hard man—some say ruthless—but he indulged his son. Young Morgan's first car was a new Cadillac convertible his father gave him for his sixteenth birthday. Perhaps because Morgan and his father were never close, his father tried to improve things by giving Morgan every material thing he could afford. He never did buy Morgan's affection.

Morgan always feared his father, even though his father had never struck him and rarely scolded him. But he had seen his father rage against business associates and the hired help and his mother. His mother trembled in his father's presence. It was because of this that Morgan hated his father. Morgan was strongly attached to his mother. The one person on earth he would die for, he was fond of saying.

His mother had a heavy gold necklace she wore every day. She'd been given it by her mother when she'd left home, and she prized it above everything else. Thus began Morgan's fondness for gold.

Morgan's mother doted on him. Before Morgan was born, she'd had two miscarriages, and Morgan's brother lived just four hours. She, too, had been part of Boston society, but was not a beauty, and married Morgan's father young, thinking he was her only chance for marital happiness. Everyone told her he was a "good man," and at the time he was becoming quite well-off. The marriage, though, was dead from the start. Morgan's father expected a wife to be more . . . well, better in bed—more "affectionate"—and he began to resent her for what he saw as her coldness toward him. He came to hate her timidity. Morgan's parents lived in the same house, but rarely spoke to each other except about household matters. After Morgan's birth they were never again sexually intimate.

Morgan's mother indulged Morgan in every way possible. To her, the sun and the moon revolved around him. To her, only his love mattered. Morgan, from an early age, could manipulate her into believing anything he wanted her to believe.

Morgan earned only mediocre grades in school and spent most of his time partying. He was kicked out of the University of Nevada, Las Vegas, for possession of marijuana and never went back to college.

Morgan Thorn from midadolescence loved women. Especially older women. Especially older rich ones, who would give him expensive gifts—gifts his parents could no longer afford. The family had fallen on hard times.

Morgan's father drank too much and, late in life, began to make bad business decisions. He had many affairs with women, usually alcoholic women, divorcees who hung around the gambling tables losing their alimony checks. He fell into depressions, and he spent most of his time in the basement, brooding and pacing. One night after supper he told his mother and son he wanted them out of the house: he had "business to take care of." When mother and son returned, there was a note on the door saying not to go in but to call the police. Morgan's father had blown his own head off with a twelve-gauge shotgun.

What was left of the estate after the creditors and lawyers got through it was only his gambling casino on the edge of town and twelve acres of nothing along a deserted stretch of highway.

Morgan was twenty-three years old at the time. His mother turned sickly after that and "lost her balance," as she put it, and never was fully right in the head again. Though she'd never loved her husband, he had been a sort of anchor in her life. The shock of his suicide and, worse, the social and financial collapse that followed was more than she could bear. One day, in a half-dazed state, she stepped in front of a Greyhound bus and died a few hours later at Mercy Hospital without regaining consciousness.

Something snapped in Morgan that night. Later, the way he put it was "It was like day became night."

He blamed his father's troubles on a banker named Sedgewick who, acting in the best interest of his bank's depositors, in a legal and ethical manner, was foreclosing on several of Morgan's father's businesses around the time of his suicide. Morgan decided Sedgewick was responsible and had to be made to pay. True, Morgan did not love his father, but he did have a strong sense of family pride. This suicide was a disgrace for the family, and it had led to his mother's accident, and Morgan was going to set that wrong right.

Morgan was patient in his revenge. He first seduced the banker's wife, then let Sedgewick know. It destroyed his marriage. Then he paid some fellows to dummy up his books so it would look to the bank examiners like Sedgewick was dipping in the till. The entire campaign took six years. Morgan finally broke into Sedgewick's house one night and set up a shotgun so it would go off when Sedgewick opened the door to the bathroom. Morgan had a perfect alibi for the time of Sedgewick's death. Hours after the shooting, Morgan went back and collected the shotgun, the very same gun that Morgan's father had used to kill himself. This crime is unsolved.

Morgan was then thirty years old.

He's been working hard, building his casino by offering cheap gas to tourists and truckers, and selling uppers, downers, and marijuana. Every so often he takes a rich widow for a ride for a few hundred thousand. He pays off the cops and politicians, and they leave him alone.

He was swindled when he bought the gold mine; his own greed got the best of him. The guy who cheated him—Dusty Thomas was his name—disappeared down in Mexico. Morgan has a man looking for him.

The Evil One's Psychology

Morgan is selfish and greedy, determined, and ruthless. He's quick-witted and cunning. And he loves gold, the sight of it, the touch of it. He secretly yearns to be in society, but at the same time revels in his reputation as a lowlife. His only hobby is seducing rich widows and divorcees. His ruling passion is to own gold, as much of it as he can. Possessing it is his only joy.

Despite himself, he sometimes has nightmares of opening a closet door and getting blasted with a shotgun. And he's hired Sedgewick's son as a pit boss in his casino to salve his conscience. The son is a heroin addict, and Morgan sees to it that he gets only the good stuff and just enough to keep him from getting the jitters.

Morgan's in love with one of his cocktail waitresses. She's married and doesn't go out with other men, and he's never so much as kissed her. She's a redhead and thin and has too many freckles and isn't pretty by most standards. He doesn't push it with her, but he aches for her. He can't put it into words, but there is a sweetness in her, a goodness, like his mother had, and that's what attracts him. Sometimes he sits at the bar and watches her work.

She and her husband live in a trailer. Her husband is on disability and drinks beer all day, and Morgan sometimes thinks he might make the guy go away sometime. She writes country-and-western songs—the soulful, old-fashioned kind best sung with a guitar-and-fiddle accompaniment—and he lets her try them out in his lounge on Monday nights when the band is off. He loves her songs. He paid a guy who supposedly knows the country-and-western business five thousand bucks to secretly take them to Nashville to try to get a record, but so far, no luck.

Is Morgan Okay as an Evil One?

Let's see. He's certainly out for himself, he's not self-sacrificing, he's not forgiving. He's been wounded (and uses it as an excuse to do evil), he's an outlaw (in the bad sense), he's clever and resourceful, and he has a special talent—for seducing women. He has sex appeal. I think he'll make a great Evil One. Now, because I want to get into his head and really feel what he feels, I'll need to write a journal in his voice.

The Evil One's Journal

I know I'm supposed to be completely honest in this, like I was talking to a shrink or something, so here goes.

I know some people think I'm a son of a bitch. They think I'm not too fussy about how I'm getting to the top, but I'll tell you true, my old man was a hell-on-wheels businessman, and he never crossed the line. You know, he never took any real risks, not the kind I'm willing to take. You've got to play the angles. If you get caught, you sometimes got to buy a judge or a cop, but that's okay. You might even have to do time, though it's not likely. If you do, you do. Guys like me, guys who can think things through, guys who aren't afraid to pressure a witness—we do what we have to do—guys like me, well, nothing can stop us. You can't let the bastards scare you. If they do, then you play by their rules. If you don't let them scare you, you can be king. You can make the rules. I make my own rules. Fear is what makes men small.

I always knew I was going to be big. I'm not there yet, but I will be. This mine thing. The gold that comes from it, I just can't sell it. I can't stand to part with it. The only thing that really gives me pleasure is to feel its cool, luminous hardness. When I touch it, it is like touching the most beautiful woman on earth. It's alive.

You want to know about Gina. The waitress. Yeah, that's hard to figure, isn't it? I don't know what to call how I feel about her. There's just something about her. She hasn't got the equipment I usually go for. I like a woman with a little flesh on her, not fat, but—you know—like Madonna. But Gina, she's skin and bones. And she's, well, maybe a little plain. But she's got this nice smile, and when she looks at you, you feel warm inside. I do, anyway. It's like she knows things. I don't know how she knows; she just knows. She came to a pal of mine's funeral. He was a good guy, like a brother to me. It was right after she started at the Paw, and I hardly knew her. She didn't say the same old muck everybody else said. She knew I was hurting, and she said it, that she knew my hurt was deep and I had to go on the best I could and not let my spirit go into the grave with my mom. She knew that's what I was feeling.

Anyway, she doesn't condemn people for what they have to do. She understands me, that's what I'm trying to say. And you know how I know it? By the way she looks at me.

You know, I got a dream. I see me back in Boston where my family came from. I see me living in a big house on a hill, going to fancy parties. And Gina is going to be there with me. She's going to dump that sack of shit she's married to one day, and I'm going to be there waiting.

About me "seducing" older women. Widows. Okay, some of them have given me some money. Some, quite a bit of money. But so what? I gave them a good time. And none of them prosecuted me for anything. . . .

So what do you think of my Evil One? I like him. He seems good and evil to me.

Note the difference in myth-based fiction from ordinary dramatic fiction. In myth-based fiction, you have a hero who will, well, act heroically. He or she acts courageously; he or she self-sacrifices; he or she is loyal; he or she is never cruel or mean for meanness's sake; and so on. The hero can, of course, be many other things. There are great varieties in the masks of the hero—he or she can be straitlaced, punctilious, fastidious, prim, or whatever—an alcoholic or drug addict, a kleptomaniac, or insane. The important thing is that, no matter what else he or she is, the hero will have heroic qualities and act heroically.

The same is true of the Evil One. The Evil One will be self-serving and determined to get that old ego satisfied no matter what. The Evil One is number one with the Evil One; no one, and nothing else, matters.

But the other qualities of the Evil One, as with the hero, can be anything. The Evil One can be man, woman, old, young, tall, short, of any ethnic background, any occupation, any temperament. The Evil One may love dogs or his or her mother; the Evil One may have a great sense of humor; he or she can be an artist, a musician, a poet, anything. The possibilities are endless, as long as the Evil One has the evil qualities.

You might say, "But gee, do I really need an Evil One? Can't I write a myth-based hero's journey in which there is no Evil One at all?" Reluctantly, I'd have to say yes—but I wouldn't recommend it.

In writing a myth-based story, it is possible to leave out a lot of the elements. You could have, as an example, a story that starts with the hero already on the journey and leave out the entire "separation" section, which happens in the hero's common-day world. You might leave out some or all of the return. A myth-based story might have no Magical Helper or Threshold Guardians. And yes, it might not have an Evil One.

I don't advise it, though. I feel that the presence of an Evil One in a story pulls the reader in with much more force. Once the reader feels the evil presence, even if the character is offstage, as in the case of most murder mysteries, the story has much more electricity.

Now then, how would you create a story without an Evil One? Even though I don't recommend it, if you feel strongly that it's best for your story, here's what you do:

Let's say, as an example, that you create a hero with a special talent; he's wounded, good at what he does for a living, and so on. Let's call him Mike. A friend of his is determined to make a dangerous ascent of the south face of Mount X. His friend faces almost certain death if he tries it alone. Mike knows that even with an expert such as he is along, the chances would still be slim. Still, he goes, acting out of self-sacrificing motives. Along the way, Mike's wound will heal at least somewhat; he might fall in love, he might have a death and rebirth—say he's trapped in a snow cave and is rescued—and so on. The story has everything you need dramatically: obstacles, character development, surprises, and so on. But it lacks an Evil One and the sheer force the Evil One can bring to a story. It is still a myth-based story.

Many pure love stories are hero's journeys without an Evil One. *My Fair Lady* (1964) is an example. Henry Higgins is certainly not an Evil One, though he shares some of the Evil One's traits. He seems only out for himself at times, to be operating to satisfy his own selfish aims, but he's not really evil.

Anyway, now that we have our hero and our Evil One, we can start to create our myth-based story, which will begin, you guessed it, with the hero at home.

4

The Home of the Brave: The Hero in the World of the Common Day

The Hero's Home

As the monomyth begins, Joseph Campbell tells us, we find the hero in the world of the common day. Campbell calls the part of the myth that happens here "separation." The hero is "separated" from his or her common-day life and leaves to go on the hero's journey: a journey of adventure, discovery, inner growth, and realization that will transform the hero forevermore.

The "separation" section of the monomyth is an important part of the story, even though the hero's transformation may not yet have begun. In the world of common day at the beginning of your tale is where you grab the reader's attention, where you, the author (as discussed at length in *How to Write a Damn Good Novel II*) will open story questions, create sympathy, empathy, and identification, and cause the reader to begin dreaming the fictive dream.

In the world of the common day, the hero is shown to have a home, friends, and family and to be part of a community. The hero, you see, has an everyday life that the reader can relate to.

Drama, Lajos Egri says in *The Art of Dramatic Writing*, is "the essence of life." And what is that essence? Struggle. Struggle in fiction is called "dramatic conflict." In *How to Write a Damn Good Novel*, chapter 2 was titled "The Three Greatest Rules of Dramatic Writing: Conflict! Conflict! Conflict!" The rules of conflict apply in any good work of fiction, in every scene, in every line of dialogue, even in the narrative. Yup, conflict! conflict! conflict! everywhere. Just as there should be chocolate in every crumb of the cake, there should be conflict, dramatic tension, struggle, strife—whatever you want to call it—everywhere, even in the world of the common day before the hero's journey begins.

All good stories are about struggle and how the struggle impacts the characters. This impact in dramatic terms is called "growth." Dramatic growth begins for the hero of myth-based fiction in the world of the common day because the conflicts begin here. Even better, as Dean Koontz says in *How to Write Best Selling Fiction* (1981), there should be "terrible trouble" right from the start.

- In *The Wizard of Oz* (1905), Dorothy's conflict with the old bat neighbor over Toto the dog comes before the tornado hits. That is an example of a wonderful conflict in the world of the common day. She's about to lose her beloved dog! Terrible trouble indeed. This action is important, too, because it has meaning for the story. She has trouble in the world of the common day, but she also has love, and that's the thing she has to come to understand at the end of her journey—

that "there's no place like home." A bit overly sentimental, but, what the hey, it's a fantasy for kids.

- In *Gone with the Wind*, Scarlett is desperately trying
  to get noticed by Ashley, the man she loves. Ashley
  has eyes only for Melanie. For Scarlett, this is terrible
  trouble.

- In *A Christmas Carol*, poor Scrooge wants only to be
  left alone, and everyone is bugging him about this
  danged Christmas stuff. He's in terrible trouble: nobody will leave him alone.

- In *The Spy Who Came in from the Cold*, Leamas the
  spy master is at the checkpoint waiting for one of his
  men to try to come over from East Berlin to the
  West. It's Leamas's world of the everyday, and it's a
  sea of troubles.

- The story of Samson and Delilah begins in the world
  of common day. He's about to be married to a Philistine, which horrifies his friends and neighbors and
  so, too, the bride's. That's terrible trouble. This is a
  Romeo and Juliet story a few thousand years before
  Shakespeare.

- Mitch McDeere, in *The Firm*, is finishing law school,
  which has been his home for quite some time. He's
  struggling to find work in the world of the common
  day: his entire future is at stake. That, for him, is
  certainly terrible trouble.

- *The Old Man and the Sea* begins in the world of the
  common day in Santiago's home village. Santiago is
  a fisherman, and he's in terrible trouble: he has not
  caught a fish in eighty-four days, and the lad he fishes
  with, the lad he is teaching to be a fisherman, is taken

from him and his "unlucky" boat. Trouble upon trouble.

- *One Flew over the Cuckoo's Nest* does not begin in McMurphy's world of the common day; it begins in the world of the common day on the psycho ward where he is about to show up. Everyone on the ward is under the heel of Big Nurse. That's terrible trouble.
- In *Jaws*, the shark starts killing immediately. The reader knows that someone is going to have to deal with this monster, so even before we meet Brody, the hero, we see there's really terrible trouble afoot.

Because the hero is in the world of the common day, the hero's struggles are usually more like our struggles; they are common-day struggles, the kinds of struggles we, the reader or viewer, might be involved in. The hero, true, is an extraordinary person, but even in that extraordinariness, there is something ordinary about him or her. Being engaged in common-day struggles is one way for the hero to connect to the reader. It proves he or she is, after all, one of us. The hero is part of a community, a part of the human family, before entering the Mythological Woods.

Before getting to Garret's terrible trouble in the world of the everyday, we'll need to first discover the premise of the story we're about to create.

The Premise of a Myth-Based Story

When mythologists talk about the construction of a myth, they talk about "functions." A function of a story is an ele-

ment of a myth: it might be a character, an event, or a physical object such as a sword or an elixir. A function might be
any clearly identifiable aspect of a myth. Functions are used
to compare one myth to another.

In describing a myth, a mythologist might say, "The hero
is burned." This is a function. Or, "The hero gets drunk."
This is a function. Or, "The hero is given a weapon." This
is also a function. Or, "The hero encounters a Fool." This is
a function too. Functions are a handy way for mythologists
to study myths, especially when making comparisons. It is
not, however, useful for writers to think that this is all there
is to creating a myth-based story. A myth-based story is not
simply a collection of functions—this leads to creating stories with no depth. A story is not simply a collection of
functions, is not simply characters in action, is not simply a
pastiche of "stuff happens."

A story emerges as a result of the dynamic forces created
by well-motivated, driven, well-rounded, dramatic characters. You can't simply follow a recipe of someone's ideal myth
and make a story out of it the way you toss flour, sugar, eggs,
and milk together to make a cake. A story is an organic,
unified whole, with each event growing out of the event that
came before. A premise is a brief statement describing that
unified whole.

In the *Damn Good Novel* books, I spent a great deal of
ink on the concept of premise because it is the most important tool in the writer's kit. Egri compared it to the chisel.
A chisel is a simple device, but without it no stone buildings
are possible, the Egyptians could not have created the pyr-
amids or the sphinx, and there would have been no Colossus
of Rhodes.

It's the same with a premise: it's the chisel that gives you the power to create a great and lasting monument.

You will need to know your premise no matter what kind of fiction you are writing. The premise is what the story is about: it is a statement of what happens to your characters as a result of the actions of your story.

That's it? you ask. Yup, that's all there is to it. Pretty simple, eh?

It's simple, but the implications of it are truly astounding. Premise is the golden key that unlocks your power and will make your myth-based story hold together as an organic unity.

Your premise statement should contain the four mighty Cs. They are:

1. Character
2. Conflict
3. Conclusion
4. Conviction (of the author)

Character means some aspect of character, or important aspect of human existence, that will test the character, such as war, love, or poverty. *Conflict* means a struggle toward some resolution with something at risk. *Conclusion* means the final state of being for the character at the end of the struggle. *Conviction* means that the author should be making a statement about life and should believe, at least in this particular circumstance involving these particular characters, that this premise has been proved.

Let's use as an example the story discussed above about the greedy businessman who goes into the desert with his wife and his assistant. The wife and the assistant are having a love affair and want the businessman's money and want him dead. So they push him off a cliff, but he miraculously survives to confront the two. Although he has a chance to kill them, he shows mercy and turns them over to the police.

This story follows the monomyth. The hero starts out in the world of common day, he's tossed into the Mythological Woods, learns the new rules, has a death and rebirth, confronts the Evil Ones, and is transformed by the experience.

What is the premise of this story?

To find a premise, you begin with the end of the story, then contrast it to the beginning and ask how the change came about.

Let's say in the end the hero has a forgiving heart. And in the beginning, he's what? Greedy, rude, bossy, mean-spirited—not a very likable hero, to say the least. So his growth is from a mean-spirited man to a forgiving one. Finally, we look at what brought about this transformation: surviving the hostile desert. How, then, might we express this story in summary? How about: a greedy, mean-spirited man manages to survive a harrowing survival experience in the desert and is transformed into a more loving, forgiving person.

That, to me, is good enough, but there are purists who like premises to be short and eloquent. You might express this as a simple equation:

Mean-spiritedness + Survival Experience = Forgiveness

Notice how mean-spiritedness indicates character, survival experience indicates conflict, and forgiveness indicates conclusion. The conviction was supplied by the author, who certainly proved the premise convincingly in this case.

This formula put as a statement might read: Struggle to survive the desert leads to forgiveness.

I don't like this quite as well because it doesn't indicate the full arc (the transformation) of the character. It leaves out the mean-spiritedness. Let's try: mean-spiritedness through a survival struggle leads to forgiveness.

Okay, that's short enough, and complete enough. If we were to write that story, this would work as a premise. Knowing your premise tells you what you need to do. You have to show (prove) that the character is mean-spirited; you have to show the survival in the desert; you have to show the hero being gradually changed; you have to show the showdown with the antagonists; you have to show the hero letting them live, which proves he forgives them.

How about a flashback showing that he has issues with his first wife left unresolved? No good—it has nothing to do with the premise.

What if he finds gold in the desert and we exploit the irony? No good—it has nothing to do with proving the premise. The premise tells you what you need to include and what you need to leave out; it is, as Lajos Egri said in *The Art of Dramatic Writing,* a "tyrant."

With a weak premise, or no premise, a story soon leaves the reader feeling that the story is out of control.

Often, in practice, you may start your story without being clear about your premise. You might write, say, what you think is an exciting opening without knowing where the story is going. That might be okay, as long as you sit back soon and ask yourself, What is this story about? What is the hero like at the beginning of the story, and what will he or she be like at the end of the story? Then ask what happens to your characters as a result of the actions of the story. And you'll have your premise.

Let's say you start a story about a couple of "good ole boys" in their late twenties who have been best pals since high school. One of them is married; the other is still single.

One day they go out fishing. They're sucking on beers, reeling in the trout, working on their Georgia tans, when somebody starts shooting at them from the shore—they think. They jump in the water and get to the opposite shore, then make their way around the lake back to their car. Nearby, they find another car and two dead guys; it looks like they killed each other. In the car, our heroes find a big bag of stolen money, say four hundred thousand dollars. They talk it over and decide to keep it. They go back to town and bury it, saying nothing. During the night, one of them goes back and digs up the money and puts it someplace else. Meanwhile, the other gets jittery and goes to the cops. They go to the spot where it was buried, and it's gone. . . .

As you can see, we have two characters and a lot of interesting action, but no premise. Why? No indication of character.

But give these actions a premise, and you might really have something.

Let's say you want to tell a story of male bonding and how it holds up under great stress—the stress of keeping all that money secret. Say that the stress of having all that money leads to the destruction of the friendship. The premise would be: sudden, ill-gotten wealth destroys friendship.

Now, knowing this, we can begin by:

- showing that our two heroes are really close friends through some self-sacrificing action (if you're going to write about friendship, the only kind worth writing about is great friendship, so that will have to be shown);
- showing that they find the money and swear it won't change their friendship;
- showing that the sudden riches put them at odds with one another in minor ways;
- showing one of them getting greedy;
- showing distrust starting to crack the bond;
- showing one of them reconciling his old wound with his dead mother (oops, that has nothing to do with the premise; we'll leave this out);
- showing them attempting to get back the friendship they see slipping away. . . .

The premise is your guide. Your tyrannical guide. It tells you what scenes you will need to have to make your organic unity. What, then, is the premise for *The Blue Light?*

The story is about Garret's ambition. The only kind of ambition worth writing about is great ambition. So what happens in the end? Her great ambition is defeated. And what defeats it? Falling in love with a gambling man as they survive an ordeal together in the desert. Premise: great love born of survival struggle defeats great ambition.

The journey she takes is, of course, into the desert, but what happens to her there is quite unexpected. She falls in love. The challenges of the adventure will put that love to the test.

To prove that premise, I'll have to show (not necessarily in this order):

- that Garret has great ambition;
- how she is pulled into the desert by that great ambition;
- how she meets her lover;
- how they fall in love;
- how they face obstacles to love and survival;
- how the course of love does not go smoothly;
- how they prove their love by risking their lives for each other;
- how she gives up her ambition for love.

These are, of course, just the broad outlines of the plot, but it is enough to get started on the stepsheet, the step-by-step plan for building a story.

In *How to Write a Damn Good Novel*, I pointed out that a story begins with a germinal idea. I then described how to proceed from that germinal idea to create dramatic characters and a stepsheet that I referred to as the "ABC's of storytelling." *In How to Write a Damn Good Novel II*, I created a few more stepsheets in order to further illustrate the concept of premise. It is my intention here to create a stepsheet showing how to incorporate mythological motif, form, structures, and heroic qualities into a story, and how to fold them together as seamlessly and slickly as Teflon on a skillet.

In creating a stepsheet for a story, I suggest you approach it with the spirit of fun. After all, here is where most of the real "creating" gets done. If you don't enjoy creating, you might be better off being an accountant. As you go, be willing to try this and try that. The creation of a story is an adventure and should be done with the spirit of adventure, full of characters you like and want to spend time with for the several months or even years you'll be working on the project. So when you go about making up your myth-based story, please enjoy, enjoy, enjoy!

Planning the Stepsheet

We'll begin, of course, in Garret's common-day world.

Garret is a reporter living in Reno, Nevada. She's single. She had an amphetamine habit, which caused her to be fired from the *New York Post*, and her terrible feelings of failure are haunting her. She could be engaged in all kinds of conflict in the world of the common day. So let's start brainstorming again.

- She could be on a story and, say, trying to pry the truth out of a reluctant politician at a committee meeting.
- She could be in conflict with her editor over a story.
- She could be in hot pursuit of a story.
- She could be lured out into the desert to be threatened with bodily harm if she kept chasing some story or other.

- Maybe she's following a story about brutal security guards at a casino.
- Or it might be a conflict in her personal life. Maybe her longtime boyfriend is making too many demands on her, and she's about to decide to break it off with him.

So how to choose? We want an exciting, dramatic opening, of course. Probably it's best to have her on the job: it would reveal more of her common-day life, show us what she is like. But her personal life is important, so let's have two conflicts going. One on the job, the other with her boyfriend—now who's he?

Let's say she broke up with Jerry, the casino shift manager, and has been going with another fellow, someone more suitable for her.

Let's see. Who might he be?

Let's say his name is Lance Packard. His father owns the Diamond Gateway Casino. Lance is nothing like his father. Lance is serious about the environment, particularly about saving Lake Tahoe from overdevelopment. What started out as a frivolous pursuit has become the only really serious thing in his life. His parents had a place on the lake while he was growing up, and he genuinely loves it and is determined that it not be further degraded by development.

That's how Garret met him, through his work at Save Lake Tahoe, his organization. She wrote a profile about him. Now, he's more serious about her than she feels comfortable with. After all, having a strong relationship interferes with her ambition. Besides, she has a deeper problem: she's afraid of being burned again. This fear she cannot admit to herself.

We need to show the hero in the world of the everyday already in conflict. This is how a myth-based story should begin.

The hero is going to be transformed by the actions of the story, as discussed above. In the beginning, the hero has a goal, usually something having to do with the hero's ruling passion. In our hero's case, this goal is to get back on a big New York paper. The hero also has an inner need, which may or may not be known to him or her. In the case of Garret, she needs a truly committed, loving relationship.

- Scrooge's goal is to keep Christmas his way, which is not to keep it at all. But he has an inner need he is unaware of—to know what made him so cold and unfeeling—and this is what the story is about, how the Ghosts of Christmas open his eyes.
- Rosie, in *The African Queen,* has a goal: she wants revenge for her brother's death. But she has an inner need for love, and the story is about how getting her revenge gets her what she really needs.
- The old man, Santiago, in *The Old Man and the Sea,* has a goal to catch a big fish. He has an inner need to regain his self-respect. He loses the fish, but gets his inner need met.
- Leamas, in *The Spy Who Came in from the Cold,* has a goal to complete a spy mission and an inner need to believe in the righteousness of his own cause; when his hopes are dashed, he chooses to die.
- Samson's goal is to smash the Philistines, the enemies of his people, but he has an inner need to be loved,

which proves to be first his undoing, then his redemption.

Let's begin our stepsheet for *The Blue Light*, keeping in mind that Garret has a goal to get back into the big leagues of her profession (her great ambition), and an inner need (which she's not fully aware of) to be loved and appreciated. I intend this story to be written in the spirit of fun, making it dramatic and exciting, but with a light, comic touch. Not quite as broadly comic as, say, *Romancing the Stone* (1984), but certainly lighter than, say, *Hamlet* (1603).

The Blue Light Stepsheet

Premise: great love born of a survival struggle defeats great ambition.

1. A Prologue.
   A couple of hormone-inflamed Reno, Nevada, teenagers are out in the desert groping each other in the back of a pickup. They're going at it pretty heavily. The girl tries to get the boy to go slow, and he's really panting. Suddenly the girl sees a weird, crystalline blue flash of light in the sky and is startled. The boy looks a moment later and sees nothing but stars. They scan the skies for a few moments and find nothing, so they return to their previous activity. The blue light appears again, more dazzling than before, a spiraling shaft of light reaching from the ground to the heavens. They both see it this time.

The boy is amazed, stupefied. He gets out of the truck bed and stares at the light, trembling with awe and fear. He thinks it's from God. She thinks the government is up to something. After a few moments, she wants to resume their merry groping, but he's fallen to his knees in prayer.

(The purpose of this prologue is to arouse the reader's curiosity about the blue light. It has no mythological function—purely a dramatic one, to foreshadow the blue light, and, well, to tell the truth, having a sexy opening never a novel hurt.)

2. We begin the hero's journey in the world of common day. Garret Holland, now twenty-eight, top reporter for the Reno *Westerner*, is driving up to a warehouse where she's supposed to meet an anonymous informant. Although she realizes she may be getting set up, she goes ahead. Ambition has clouded her judgment. She's working on a story about an organized gang that's ripping off casinos and winners; she knows there's an inside man and wants his identity. Accosted by the crooks, who want her off the story, she pulls out a can from her jacket and douses them with itching powder. By promising to give them the antidote, she gets the information she wants. Afterward, she says she's really sorry, but there is no antidote. They rush off. We see now that she's courageous and clever and resourceful and, like most heroes, has that old swelled head called hubris.

3. It's the next morning. Garret is at her desk in the news room, finishing up her story. Lance Packard

shows up. She's just broken up with him—he committed the unpardonable sin: he went and "got serious" on her. She is fond of him, but a serious relationship would interfere with her great ambition, and she can't have that. He accuses her of being afraid of commitment—isn't it the guys who are supposed to be afraid of that? The reader should sense that she's been wounded in the past and that, beneath her impregnable defenses, she really is afraid.

4. Later, Garret stops by the other editor's office, the avuncular Marion Weibel. He wants her to back away from her hard-hitting story: the man she's named is a dangerous psychopath. The editor lectures her about taking too many risks. The reader will see she's a heroic character in that she's good at what she does for a living. Hopefully, we'll get the sense that she's willing to cross lines other reporters are not willing to cross, that she's something of a maverick, an outlaw.

Okay, we've got a good start.

Next, her editor will offer Garret an assignment to go into the desert to find out about the mysterious blue light. This is her call to adventure.

So we've shown Garret's common-day world before she gets her call to adventure. We've gotten to know her and her life before the call that will mark the beginning of a journey of transformation. The important aspects of the hero and the hero's past—that he or she is good at what he or she does for a living, possesses a special talent, is wounded, is courageous, is clever and resourceful, and so on—should be shown by now. But don't try to shoehorn them in if they don't come out in the course of the actions you've created. If you miss some aspects of the hero's character or fail to reveal some important event in the hero's past, don't worry about it—it will be revealed later.

The Call to Adventure

The call to adventure normally comes from a character known as the "Herald."

The Herald is simply a character who brings the call to adventure to the hero. The Herald of old was usually a messenger of the king who brought word to the knight that the king had a mission for him. The Herald may be a secretary, a cop, a computer—virtually any character or thing that will signal the hero's call to adventure.

Remember the mama pig giving money to the three little pigs and sending them out into the world where the wolf would huff and puff and blow their houses down? The giving of the money is the call to adventure.

Remember Little Red Ridinghood's mama giving her the basket to take to Grandma's house? That's her call to adventure.

The arrival of the invitation to the ball at Cinderella's house is her call to adventure.

When M calls James Bond to his office to give him an assignment, he is giving him his call to adventure.

In *Jaws*, Police Chief Brody is summoned to look at a body on the beach: that's his call to adventure.

On the old TV show *Mission Impossible*, the call to adventure was a tape recording that would self-destruct after the assignment was given. The voice on that tape recorder, therefore, is the Herald.

In a private detective story, the Herald is usually the client. In a spy story, the spy is controlled by a spy master, who gives the spy his mission: the spy master or his subordinate is the Herald. The Herald may not even be a person or a tape recording of a person. The hero, say, gets hit on the head with a brick one day on the way home from work and wakes up an amnesiac. The brick functions as the Herald.

The call to adventure in a mythic story should not be confused with the "inciting incident" that occurs in a dramatic story. A dramatic story begins in what is called the "status quo" situation, which is often, but not always, the hero's world of the common day. The dramatic events are set in motion by what is called the inciting incident, which may or may not be a call to adventure. In other words, the inciting incident may call the hero to go on a journey, or it may not; it may simply start a chain of dramatic events in which the hero stays put in the world of common day.

There are, of course, dramatic stories that do not have a hero as the protagonist. There are villain-as-protagonist dramatic stories, and antihero-as-protagonist dramatic stories, neither of which are myth based, though there may be many common elements.

Answering the Call to Adventure

The call to adventure is sometimes irresistible. The hero may be shanghaied, as an example—knocked on the head with a billy club, and have no choice in the matter. He or she is going off on the journey and that's that.

If the call to adventure is not irresistible, the hero has two choices: he or she can say, "Okay, I'm on my way," or "Hell no, I won't go." If the hero answers the call to adventure with an "Okay, I'm on my way," the following happens:

- The hero may get advice for the journey from the Wise One, sometimes called the "Mentor." The Wise One is always an old person, full of wisdom to the brim. This person may be man or woman, spirit, owl, spaceman, android, whatever—as long as he or she is old and wise.

- The hero may get some magic to take along on the journey from a Magical Helper. The Magical Helper in ancient myths would give the hero a magical potion or amulet to help him succeed in his mission. A Magical Helper in a modern myth-based story may have real magic or may have modern technomagic, such as Q in the James Bond series. The Magical Helper and the Wise One may be the same character. It's okay to give more than one function to a character; myth-based fiction is as flexible as a garden hose.

- The hero may get weapons for the journey from the Armorer (who may also be the Wise One, the

Threshold Guardian, the Loved One, and so on).
These weapons may be guns and knives and rockets,
or they may be other weapons. In the war of love,
weapons may be, say, a fancy gown and a new hairdo
for the female hero, who is going to the ball in hopes
of charming the prince, or a great business suit and
serious glasses if she's to charm the board of directors
of her company. Weapons are simply implements for
the hero to use along the way to win victory. Q in
the James Bond stories is the Magical Helper and the
Armorer as well.

- The hero may make preparations for the journey:
  packing gear, securing transportation, etc. "Get the
  Batmobile ready, Robin!"
- The hero may recruit others, such as the Sidekick, to
  take along on the journey. The Sidekick is a close
  friend and associate of the hero. The Sidekick has all
  the qualities of the hero, including having a special
  talent, being good at what he or she does for a living,
  and so on, but the Sidekick is usually not wounded
  and is usually not quite as gifted as the hero. Take
  Batman and Robin. Robin is good in a fight, clever,
  resourceful, and courageous, but he is not Batman.
  Little John (of the Robin Hood legend) is good in a
  fight, loyal, courageous, clever, and resourceful, but
  he's no Robin Hood. Only Robin Hood can split the
  arrow in the bull's-eye at five hundred feet. If you're
  in trouble, Tonto would be a good guy to have at
  your side, but the Lone Ranger is a shade better
  shot—and has silver bullets in his gun (it's doubtful
  that they're better, but it sounds good). Pancho is

great in a brawl, but, again, the Cisco Kid is a tad better.

The same is true for the Sidekick in less cartoonish forms of popular fiction. Hawk (in the Robert B. Parker books) is good in a fight, but he's no Spenser when it comes to solving a crime. Dr. Watson is a good man and certainly heroic, but he hasn't the genius of Sherlock Holmes. Paul Drake is a good PI, but when it comes to finding out who really killed Mrs. Quigley in the quagmire, you'd better call Perry Mason.

- The hero may encounter the Lover in the world of common day, who may accompany the hero on the journey. The Sidekick and the Lover may be the same character, as in *The African Queen*.

- The hero may have a tearful parting with a Loved One. This character may be a mother, father, sweetheart, or close friend. The character usually appears at the end of the story in a happy reunion. This tearful parting, of course, gains sympathy for the hero and shows that a personal sacrifice is being made in order to go on the journey. The Loved One of the Tearful Good-bye is a minor character.

- The hero may be advised by the Threshold Guardian not to go on the journey. Threshold Guardians are fascinating mythological characters because they are always weak. Weak characters usually are not well suited for dramatic works, but the Threshold Guardian is always weak, illogical as it may sound. The Threshold Guardian warns the hero that the journey has dangers, but the hero always ignores the warning.

The Threshold Guardian stands in the way of the hero but for a moment. Threshold Guardians usually appear just before the start of the journey or just after the journey has begun. They may also appear at the later threshold, which marks the beginning of the hero's return, to advise the hero not to go back to the world of the common day. Occasionally they will appear along the path of the journey to warn the hero that danger lies ahead. Although heroes never heed them, they often flummox other characters, even causing panic.

Note: The Threshold Guardian may be fused with the Wise One or the Loved One of the Tearful Good-bye, as discussed above. In other words, the same character may be the Loved One giving the tearful good-bye and at the same time warning the hero against making the journey. It's possible for most of the mythological cast of characters to be fused with one another, so that the characters play more than one role, just as in real life. Sometimes you play the Wise One giving advice to a friend; sometimes you're a Threshold Guardian telling your friend not to take that job in Detroit. Other times you play the Armorer, giving your neighbor enough phenol methylcarbonate to kill every cockroach in his outhouse.

Some of the mythological cast members often found in the world of common day may not be encountered until later in the story. They may also appear in the world of common day and appear later as well. Despite what you may have heard or read, there are no fixed rules about when and where or how often we may meet this or that mythological character. The Loved One of the Tearful Good-bye, as mentioned, is often seen again in the end, when there is a tearful reunion with the hero. The Wise One and the Sidekick might accompany the hero on the journey. The Hero's Lover may be encountered in the world of common day or, later, on the journey itself.

If the Hero Refuses the Call

Ah, you say, but what if the hero says, "Hell no, I won't go!" What then?

If the hero refuses the call, Campbell tells us, "The subject loses the power of affirmative action and becomes a victim to be saved. His flowering world becomes a wasteland of dry stones and life feels meaningless. . . ."

Pressure will be brought to bear on the hero by friends, loved ones, officialdom, the community, and so on, to answer the call. If the hero still doesn't answer, that pressure will cause the hero to begin to degenerate, socially, morally, and psychologically.

Perhaps the best-known example of the hero refusing the call to adventure is the Humphrey Bogart character, Rick, in the film *Casablanca* (1942). As the hero, he's supposed to fight the Nazis. But he's determined to stay out of politics. His friends start to pressure him, he becomes irritable, he drinks, he loses status and respect. In the end, of course, he gives up the woman he loves to help the anti-Nazi cause and goes off to join the Free French. It is a story of a man reluctantly becoming a hero.

If Rick had not joined the fight in the end, he would have been an antihero. Antiheroes are not villains. Antiheroes are simply candidates for herodom who refuse the call.

Another great old film, *Sergeant York* (1941), starring Gary Cooper, was supposedly the true story of Alvin York, a farmer from Tennessee who became the most decorated American soldier of World War I. His call to adventure is a draft notice. He refuses—on moral grounds. He's a Christian pacifist. He's assailed as a coward and turncoat by friends and family in his community, he gets into fights, he drinks. . . . He disintegrates until the Wise One (his pastor, played to the hilt by Walter Brennan) convinces him that his pacifist views are actually not in line with the teachings of the Bible and that he is obligated to fight evil. So, after a tearful parting with his betrothed (the Loved One) and his ma (Loved One #2), off he goes on his journey.

The demonstration stepsheet above lists the steps up to the point where Garret is to receive her call to adventure. A stepsheet is, remember, a tentative plan for a story. A story must be drafted, rewritten, rewritten, rewritten, and polished, polished, polished before it is done. Your plans might change. As an example of how the stepsheet translates into the story, I offer the following:

THE BLUE LIGHT
a novel
by James N. Frey

Prologue

The stars were amazing that night, covering the velvet blackness of the sky like diamond dust. There was no moon. The desert was quiet, except for the sound of an old pickup going along a rutted road, its headlights dancing in the night. The pickup came to a stop at the edge of a ravine, and the young man at the wheel shut off the engine. He bent over and kissed the girl sitting next to him, and then he got out and went around to the passenger's side and opened the door. The girl got out, slowly, shyly. Tentatively. He kissed her again, his arms around her, gently drawing her to him. She put her arms around him and mussed his hair playfully.

He laughed.

He wore jeans and cowboy boots and a sweatshirt he'd borrowed from his older brother that was too big for his lean, muscular frame. She, too, wore jeans, but she had on a flannel shirt that buttoned down the front. She had long, dark hair, and was a little plump, and would probably get much plumper as the years went by.

The girl took a blanket out of the truck and handed it to him. It was a horse blanket and smelled of the horse and leather and liniment, familiar smells to both of them. The boy walked up a small rise where the sage grass was thick and smelled sweetly.

She followed behind him and helped him spread the blanket on the grass. They knelt on the blanket, looking at each other and holding each other's hands for a long moment, ignoring the splash of diamond dust in the heavens above them.

They'd seen an actor and actress face each other on their knees in a movie before they started making love, so they thought it was the right thing to do. The boy's big brother had told him that girls always wanted it slow and easy. It was hard, but that was the way to please them, and if you didn't please them, they didn't want to pleasure you no more, he'd said.

A cool breeze brushed her long hair. She took a paper bag out of a pocket and opened it and took out a small foil package and a tube of lubricant and put it on the blanket.

He smiled, and they lay down on the blanket, holding hands and looking up at the sky, and saw the stars for the first time. After a moment she whispered that it was almost as if they were with the stars. He stroked her hair and rose on one elbow and started kissing her. She whispered that she wanted him to love her always, and he said that he would. His brother had told him about that, too.

They kissed for a long while, and then he unbuttoned her shirt and started kissing her soft, fleshy breasts above her bra, and she started to breathe more deeply . . . and then suddenly she sat up and told him to look at the sky.

He turned and looked, but saw nothing there.

"What was it?" he asked.

"A light flickered; it was awesome."

"What kind of a light?"

"A blue light. It was like . . . shimmering."

They scanned the sky for a few seconds.

"Ain't no light now," the boy said.

"It was really something," the girl said.

The boy lay back down. "Hey," he said, patting the blanket. "Where were we?"

She joined him, putting her arms around his neck. "I really did see something," she said.

"Okay. Now I'm going to show you something," he said.

He kissed her, and she drew him to her tightly. They were soon rolling around on the blanket, laughing and tickling each other. He grasped her shirt with both hands and pulled it off her shoulders. She giggled and grabbed for his belt, unbuckling it, jerking it.

Suddenly she sat up again, pointing toward the sky. "Look! Look!"

They both saw it now, a shaft of brilliant light shimmering before them. Inside the iridescent blue shaft, it looked like glowing crystals pulsating.

The boy scrambled to his feet, standing before it, trembling. The girl stood next to him, putting her shirt back on.

"What do you think it is?" she asked.

"The tribulation," he said, falling to his knees. "Lord, save us! Lord, take us now! Lord, forgive us our sins!"

And then the light shut off, as it had before.

The stars twinkled silently above them against the black sky.

After a while the girl went back to the blanket, folding it around herself. "Come, keep me warm," she said.

But the boy didn't move; he just kept saying the Lord's Prayer over and over and over again. After a while, he stopped, and they got back in the pickup and headed back to town.

Chapter 1

She called herself by her middle name, Garret. Garret Holland. A hotshot newshound, as she liked to call herself. She was a reporter for the Reno *Westerner* and at the moment was pulling up in front of an old warehouse on Lake Street in Reno.

The street was empty. It was a dark, moonless night. The warehouse was set back from the street, surrounded by a chain-link fence with razor wire on top. The grass was overgrown, and there were papers and cans and bottles all over the place. A sign in the window said FOR LEASE.

Goddamn perfect place for some bad business, she thought.

She stopped her car in front of the office. It was eleven o'clock. She rolled down the window of her old Toyota Camry. A cool, dry breeze off the desert blew in. She listened. All she could hear was the sound of traffic on the freeway a block away. Her stomach felt tight. She put a Tums in her mouth and sucked on it.

Relax and focus, her street-fighting teacher, Rufus Giardello, had taught her back in New York. Relax and focus. She breathed deeply, running through Rufus's drill in her head: scream "NO," kick 'em in the crotch, go for the eyes. That's what Rufus taught. Simple, direct, and you didn't have to wear gees as in other martial arts. If all else fails, Rufus said, bite your attacker in the throat and rip his fucking jugular out. His students trained by bitting grapefruit. Rufus lacked finesse, but his methods had proven useful more than once. Not that Garret had bitten anyone. Or kicked anyone either, for that matter.

She checked the building perched on a small hill across the street. A commercial print shop. Nobody around that she could see.

Well, star reporter, she thought, *this is what you get the big bucks for.*

The anonymous caller who'd phoned her earlier had said she had important information about a gang who was ripping off casino winners. She said she had some photos of the head man. Garret had been writing about the gang for a month now, and still there had been no arrests. It felt right, what the woman said on the phone. And there was fear in her voice. If she was acting, she was good at it.

Still, Garret thought, *it would be best, like a good Boy Scout, to be prepared.*

She got out of the car and stood in the light of a street lamp. Garret, just a month past her twenty-eighth birthday, was thin, lithe, athletic, five-foot five. Her movements were quick, with a dancer's grace. She had sandy blonde hair, cut in an easy-to-care-for bob, and cool, ice blue eyes that seemed constantly searching. She had a straight nose and a small mouth with perfect teeth. No makeup. She wore gray slacks and a practical, tan, tweed blazer.

She opened the trunk and took out an old army jacket she had fitted out for just such an occasion. She took off her blazer and put on the army jacket. It was heavy and pinched her shoulders. The can of pepper spray cut into her hip, or maybe it was the sack of marbles she used as a blackjack. She let out a deep breath and switched on her pocket tape recorder, slipped it into her inside pocket, and closed her trunk. Show time.

She took a deep breath and started up the walk, holding the heavy barrel flashlight in her hand, feeling like the heroine of a cheap horror film heading for the attic where the spooky noises were coming from. *Relax and focus.* The gang was vicious. They'd beaten some of their victims severely, but they had never used guns, and she knew why: the courts in Nevada don't take a friendly view of gun crimes. She never used a gun either. She wasn't comfortable with firearms. More people got shot with their own guns than ever stopped a bad guy.

The door to the office opened. Garret shined her flashlight on the doorway, revealing the figure of a woman, waving to her.

"This way," the woman said, withdrawing back inside. "Hurry!"

Garret gripped the flashlight tighter. Her heart beat quickly; electricity tingled up her spine.

She got to the end of the walk and found the door ajar.

"Hello?" she said.

"Come in," the woman said, her voice trembling.

Garret pushed the door open and shined the light inside. A woman stood in the middle of the room, her arm covering her face.

"Close the door; I don't want to be seen."

Garret bit down on the Tums and stepped in and closed the door behind her.

Suddenly the light came on, and she found herself facing two men wearing ski masks. The woman, crouching low and hiding her face, scooted behind Garret and out the door.

"Sorry . . . ," she said to Garret as she passed by.

"Fink," Garret managed.

Her throat closed up.

Garret turned to the two men. One, over six feet, went at least three hundred. The other man was shorter, five-nine or ten, and had what looked like a shortened baseball bat in his hand.

"Ah, good evening, gentlemen," she said. "Let me guess—the Garret Holland Fan Club."

"You're here to be taught a lesson," the smaller man said. He had a low voice, soft. *Probably a good singer,* Garret thought.

The man said, "You'll write no more shit about us. We don't like all this heat we been takin' on account of you."

"You got a deal. Okay, well, I've got to go now."

"First we got to see you been punished." They moved toward her.

She backed away, coming up against a desk. "Let me warn you, my paper knows where I am, and if I don't report in in five minutes, the cops are going to be swarming all over the place."

"Then," the smaller man said to the bigger one, "we'd better work quick."

The big man chuckled. She didn't see anything funny.

They were a few feet from her. She drew a can of mace from her jacket. The shorter one swung his club and knocked the can out of her hand, and it clattered across the floor.

"Oh, shit!" she said. Then, as he came closer, she yelled, "NOOOOOO!" and kicked at his groin, but he twisted at the last moment and took the blow in the thigh. He grabbed her leg and yanked it upward, spilling her over the top of the desk onto the floor, banging her head. Stars danced in her head. The big man loomed above her. He chuckled again.

She rolled and crawled quickly away, snatching her foot away from the big man's hand as he grabbed for her. She scrambled to her feet and vaulted a desk and raced toward the door.

The smaller man blocked her way, and the big man was coming up behind her. "You ain't had your lesson yet," he said.

"Okay, you want to play hardball," she said, jerking another can from her jacket. "Poof!" A cloud of powder covered him as she swung around and doused the big man with the same.

The two men stood there for a moment looking at her. The big man started to laugh, then suddenly started tearing at his clothes, scratching himself all over.

"Christ!" the smaller one screamed. The other yelped like a kicked dog.

She backed away toward the wall, watching them hop around, squealing, cursing, scratching like mad.

She held a can out in front of her. "The antidote, gentlemen. Give me your leader, and you get to have all you want." She sprayed a bit of it into the air.

The big man yelled, "Tell her! Oh, God, I can't stand it."

"Stand over there," she told them both. "Against the wall."

The big man hopped over to the wall. The other man was rolling on the floor, begging, "Please, oh, please, help me, oh, God, help me, please."

She said, "A name, and it better be right, because I already know who it is; I just want confirmation."

"B-Benny Sodder," he managed. "Runs a bar out at the lake."

"Try again."

"Please, I can't stand it!" He was clawing at his skin; blood smeared his tattered shirt.

"Give him up; I'll cool your skin."

"Harry Ballard!"

"Okay, that's more like it."

She headed for the door.

"The antidote!" he screamed.

"This can? It's for athlete's foot. For the itch, plain water and lots of soap will do it," she said. "Suggest you hurry."

They raced past her on the sidewalk and ran down the street, throwing off their clothes.

Rufus would have been proud, she thought. *Show no mercy,* he always said.

The next morning at her desk, Garret gulped strong French-roast coffee. She hadn't gotten home until after midnight and hadn't slept well. *Too much adrenaline,* she thought. The phone rang.

"Holland," she answered.

"Sweetheart, I've got to see you; we have to talk."

She swallowed, but said nothing.

"Sweetheart, please."

"Lance, I said everything the other night that needs to be said."

"But, sweetheart, we were meant for each other. . . ."

"Lance, please, don't."

"You know what I think. I think you're chicken."

"Have it your way."

"We've got real chemistry; I know it. It's that you're already married—to that damn job. I'm glad you love your work, honest. I'm sorry if I groused a bit too much about it. I know you love it."

"Listen, Lance, it's over. Kaput. Finished."

"I need you desperately, sweetheart."

"Sorry." She hung up the phone.

She took a deep breath. It wasn't easy. She was fond of him. Only . . . only he wanted all of her, and she wasn't willing to give all of her. She had other plans, to get back to the East Coast, to get out of this hick town, to get with a big paper, a paper that made a damn difference.

At 9:10 she filed her story, and fifteen minutes later Lenny Fargo, the *Westerner*'s assistant editor, stuck his head in the door. He was an old-timer, slowing down for retirement. He looked at her over the top of his glasses.

"Mr. Big wants to see you." Mr. Big was the editor, Marion Weibel.

"He read my copy? He didn't like it?"

"He didn't say."

She put her purse in the bottom drawer of her desk, brushed some lint off her pants suit, ran her hand through her hair, put some drops in her eyes to get the red out, and dabbed on a little lipstick.

"Am I beautiful?" she asked Lenny Fargo.

"Always."

"Okay, let's go."

The two of them crossed the city room. Most of the half-dozen reporters were out covering their assignments. Only Fred Hanson, the new kid just out of Berkeley journalism school, was still at his computer. He looked up as they passed his desk—he didn't yet rate a cubicle. "Dragged to the principal again?" he asked her.

"You got to take your whippins in this business."

She was only a few years older than Fred, but she'd been a reporter, she was fond of telling him, for a hundred years longer.

Lenny knocked at the editor-in-chief's office, and the two walked in.

Marion Weibel sat behind a desk piled with papers. He was an obese man in his forties. He had a round, florid face, and wore thick, black-rimmed glasses. He reached for a piece of red licorice as they entered the room and gestured for them to have some. Garret took one.

"I read your story, Garret."

"I have more than one source; I carefully checked the facts."

"I've got no quarrel with the job you did—it's something else. Lenny, leave us alone, would you?"

Lenny Fargo nodded and shuffled out of the room.

Garret dropped into a chair and sucked on the licorice.

"When I was a pup," Weibel said, "this Harry Ballard character owned a body shop south of town. Some say he was running stolen cars down to Mexico. Some say he once killed a man in a knife fight. Not exactly a fair fight."

"All the more reason for us to nail the bastard."

"And what if he comes after you—or me?"

"I'm not scared, are you?"

He took out a handkerchief and wiped his forehead. "What do you say we cut his name out of the story, Garret?"

"No."

"We're taking an awful chance."

"It's a risky business, didn't your mother tell you? That all? I've got a dog show to attend."

"I've got to think about this," he said.

"You're the boss."

"It's a mighty fine piece," he said. "You sure got the knack for stringing words together."

"Thanks for that," she said. "And thanks for the licorice."

Marion Weibel heaved his weight in his chair. "Hold it a minute, Garret."

She did. "Yes?"

He rubbed his chin. "Look," he said, "I know why you knock yourself out, and it isn't just because you're a hot rod."

"I do my job, the way it should be done."

"Yeah. Listen. You were the youngest, brightest reporter they ever had at the *New York Post,* and they dumped you because you were into taking speed."

Garret felt a catch in her throat. Another editor, another office, flashed in front of her mind's eyes, and the words *You have cast a shadow on the integrity of this paper, and we can no longer tolerate your employment.*

This editor now said, "I just want you to know I understand why you take such risks."

"I never hid the fact I was hooked on amphetamines. Past tense. Any time you want me to pee in a bottle, just say the word."

"Christ, I know you kicked 'em. And I know your old man was a big-shot reporter at the old *Herald Tribune* and later at *Newsweek,* some place like that, and you feel you've got to be in the big time or you're a nobody. I know you want to get back on the fast track. I know you want to do work that will shine, casting light all the way to the East Coast, and I'll help you do it—so long as we're not ducking bullets around here."

"Haven't been shot yet."

"Look, kid, I like you. I just want you not to kill yourself just to get ahead. There's no point in being the best reporter in the cemetery."

"I'll try to remember that, Marion. Thanks."

"One more thing. I've got an assignment here that might take a few days. Could be a big story."

"What is it?"

"South of here, there've been reports of a strange blue light in the sky."

"UFOs again? Christ, Nevada has more UFOs than the Sahara has sand."

"Don't know what it is. Maybe it's a giant hoax. Could be a big story."

"Marion, I don't like the desert much. I get sunburned really easily. Can't you give this one to the kid?"

"Okay, but the only other thing I've got is the meeting of the sewer committee."

"Sand or sewers. I'll take sewers; at least the city council is air-conditioned."

Okay, there we have the opening of the novel. So far, I like her.

Now to continue the stepsheet. Garret has just gotten her call to adventure, the assignment from her editor to go into the desert and check out this weird blue light, and she has refused the call. We know what happens to heroes who refuse the call: they begin to deteriorate.

Garret's Stepsheet Continues

5. Her editor gives her the assignment to check out the blue light. This is her call to adventure, and she refuses the call.

6. Garret goes to the sewer meeting. It's too dull to endure. She becomes irritable, feeling guilty for turning down an assignment. *(The hero begins to deteriorate.)* On her way home, she listens to a radio talk show. Callers are saying the light has magical qualities; one claimed it cured his warts. She sees there may be a big story in it, and, damn it! somebody else is getting it. She stops at a bar to have a drink and throw darts against guys for money. She wins a few bucks. The blue light is on the news: a psychic is saying it's the end of the world; a man claims he saw the Virgin Mary in it; another, that the light is coming from a spaceship. It's drawing attention from around the globe. She gets a little schnockered, deteriorating further. *(The hero has a change of consciousness.)* A handsome fellow buys her a drink. He's from the East, went to Harvard, and she's delighted to meet him, but it's quickly obvious that he's shallow and not for her. In a long, boring monologue about himself, he keeps saying that the one thing he learned at Harvard that has served him well is, if you want something, go and get it and don't take no for an answer.

7. It's the next morning. She goes to Fred Hanson's

apartment, determined to get the blue light assignment from him. She bamboozles Fred into believing
that it is not the right assignment for him, but that
it would be perfect for her. He gives her the short-
wave radio the boss gave him, thanking her. She
calls her editor, secures the assignment, and promises him a great story.

8. Garret prepares for her journey into the Mythological Woods. In her apartment building there's an old
lady, Dolly Anderson, a desert rat. Garret goes to
see her for advice. *(The hero visits the Wise One.)*
Dolly gives her maps and a compass, lots of water
bottles, a snake-bite kit, and so on. The Wise One,
acting as a Threshold Guardian, warns her not to
go. (Remember, a mythological character may play
more than one role.) The blue light is coming from
an area of the desert called Hogan's Maze. In the
nineteenth century, a prospector named Hogan
found a big gold strike out there and never told anyone where it was. Many have gone looking for it
and have seen ghosts and spirits and, since the
1950s, a lot of UFO activity. Many men have gone
into Hogan's Maze (an area honeycombed with canyons, mesas, drifting sand dunes, high winds, and
dry creek beds) and have never come back. Because
of metal deposits in the rock, compasses are thrown
off; streams change their course; there are many dust
storms; maps are unreliable.

Garret assures Dolly she'll be okay. She's got a
good sense of direction; she could even find her way
around Boston with half a toot on. This is some-

thing she has to do, she says—there might just be a big story out there, and she's just the guy who can land it. *(The hero has hubris.)* The Wise One gives her an old map that shows where there might be water and gives her advice on finding shade, cutting into barrel cactus, and so on. She tells her to keep a knife in her boot. And that her SUV doesn't have enough ground clearance. Garret needs a Land Rover, or something like it, a real desert yacht, and offers her hers, but Garret turns it down because it has no air-conditioning.

9. Garret visits Ida Day, who runs a women's self-defense shop. *(The hero visits the Armorer.)* She buys some stuff for self-defense and thanks Ida for the itching powder.

Okay, for Garret the first part of the hero's journey, the *separation,* is over; now she crosses the threshold and begins her *initiation.*

To recap what has happened so far:

Garret began doing what most heroes do: she was in conflict in the world of common day—the kind of conflicts she routinely engaged in. I showed her as part of a community; I showed her apartment, her job, her everyday life. I hope the reader can relate to her everyday life, even though her everyday life is a tad more exciting than the lives that most of us are blessed with. She is, after all, a *homo fictus,* a species that always has more exciting lives. Then she received her call to adventure from her editor boss (the Herald) and did what reluctant heroes do—she said, "Hell, no."

When heroes say no, they start to disintegrate. Garret, as

indicated on the stepsheet, will disintegrate and drink, having a change of consciousness. She will finally say yes, and then she will go to the Wise One/Threshold Guardian and to the Armorer and make preparations for the journey.

But notice, please, that she will not get help from a Magical Helper, will not take on a Sidekick, and did not have a tearful parting with a Loved One, nor meet the Hero's Lover. The hero's journey is quite flexible. Use what you need, what comes naturally out of the character's motives and actions, and leave the rest. Don't insert things just because they fit the paradigm. We are not making cookie-cutter stories. We're creating new, myth-based stories that are wholly modern and original.

However, because they resonate so strongly with readers, it might be a good idea to see if the mythological characters and motifs would fit in to my story. One of my students was writing a myth-based detective novel without a Wise One. When I pointed this out to her, she asked who the character might be. I said I didn't know, that she should dream one up.

The character she dreamed up was an old curmudgeon policewoman, who turned out to be absolutely delightful and enriched the novel greatly.

So before I move on, perhaps I'd better consider my alternatives. Let's see.

I'm satisfied for now that I have the right characters and motifs and my story is on track. Garret's ready to cross the threshold and enter the Mythological Woods, which, in this case, is the desert. To her, it is certainly a strange place full of fabulous forces where she will indeed be tested.

The reader knows the first part of the premise: that this

is a story about a hero on her journey, a hero with great ambition. Later, we'll see how that ambition holds up when confronted by love. But first there are other mythological characters to be met on the journey; they are the subject of the next chapter.

5

The Woods Are Full of Fascinating Characters

The Hero's Lover

The hero crosses the threshold, leaves the world of common day, and we have the second part of the hero's journey, the "initiation," which takes place in the "Mythological Woods" or the "Dark Woods." In these woods, the hero is apt to run into a host of fascinating mythological characters. The Evil One has already been discussed, and there will be a further discussion of the Evil One when the hero has a confrontation with the Evil One's vile self further along on the journey.

In the Mythological Woods, the hero is likely to encounter a character Hollywood calls the "love interest." The Hero's Lover. Of course you can cook up a fine, myth-based story without this character, but if the hero has a lover, he or she will likely be an important character in the story.

First, the Hero's Lover is not a helpmate. The Hero's Lover is an antagonist; that is, a character standing in the way of the hero's goals and desires, just like any other antagonist. There will be dramatic conflict with this character and lots of it.

The road of love in fiction is always full of potholes. In real life, too, I'm told.

Any good Hero's Lover, of course, will be a total opposite to the hero; in other words, the character will be well orchestrated with the hero.

Some examples of well-orchestrated characters:

- In *The African Queen,* Rosie and Charley are well orchestrated. She's an uptight spinster, clean, organized, neat and proper, a teetotaler; he's a besotted river rat, dirty, disorganized, sloppy, and irreverent.
- Scarlett, the hero of *Gone with the Wind,* is a young, naive fluff head, concerned only with trivial pursuits involving society balls and flirting with young gentlemen. Her lover, Rhett Butler, is worldly, cynical, antisocial, and, in her view, "no gentleman."
- In *Lolita,* Humbert Humbert is worldly, a jaded romantic, middle-aged, educated, and sophisticated; Lolita is young, snippy, ignorant, and spoiled.
- Samson is immensely strong, a rube, inexperienced in the ways of the world, naive, childlike, open, honest. Delilah is sophisticated, experienced, alluring, and dishonest.
- Leamas, in *The Spy Who Came in from the Cold,* is jaded, over-the-hill, a burned-out spy, in search of something to believe in; his lover, Liz, is young, naive, a devoted communist, a true believer.
- In *The Godfather,* Michael Corleone is a killer, a

crime lord, cunning and ruthless; his love, Kay, is a
sweet, naive kindergarten teacher.

In creating the Hero's Lover, then, you should keep in
mind that you want to make them opposites. All the major
characters should be well orchestrated, but with the Hero's
Lover, it is particularly critical.

Characters who are well orchestrated will have conflict at
many different levels. Take my wife and me as an example.
She's something of a culture vulture: she was an art history
major in college, then later studied four more years for a
degree in music. She sings in the San Francisco Bach Choir.
She's quiet and soft-spoken, keenly intelligent, a pleasant
person to be around, rarely in a bad mood, mostly up-beat,
loving, and kind. I majored in experimental psychology and
did graduate work in English literature, don't know a Van
Gogh from a Degas, and am tone-deaf. I'm rather outgoing,
outspoken—some say opinionated and overbearing—
moody, and love writing, socializing with writers, sailing,
and reading. She's thrifty—I'm a, well, let's say, I'm not
thrifty. She likes sappy romances; I like gripping suspense
stories. She likes her little Saturn; I drive a beat-up old
pickup truck. And on and on, into the night.

When we go traveling, as an example, she wants to see
the museums and cathedrals, the palace gardens, the dining
rooms of fancy hotels. I want to see the boat harbors and
the beer gardens and dives and hangouts of the working
stiffs. She likes a fine cabernet with her foie gras and I like
stout German lager with a hunk of coarse bread and a spicy
sausage.

So how, you wonder, have we managed to get along for lo these many years?

I guess it's my high level of tolerance, open-mindedness, and ability to compromise.

If characters are not well orchestrated, the work becomes flat. No sparks will fly. You'll have conversations, not conflict; dullness, not drama.

Okay, then, how do you go about creating the Hero's Lover?

First thing: think orchestration. Make the Hero's Lover opposite the hero in as many ways as possible.

As an example, let's find a well-orchestrated Hero's Lover for *The Blue Light.*

Garret's Lover

Okay, then, we'll need a character who is well orchestrated to our hard-driving, overly ambitious, careerist Garret Holland.

First, let's give him a name.

Fred.

Naw, sounds a little ordinary. So do Jim, Bill, Bob. . . . Let's try:

Quint.

Okay, the lover's name is Quint. Quint what?

How about Quint Laudermilk?

He sounds like a high-society type of person, which is what Garret is, and we're looking for opposites.

How about Quint Jones?

To me, this suggests a rather blue-collar character, a grease-under-the-fingernails kind of guy, just right for this novel, well orchestrated with Garret, who went to Yale, is the daughter of a socialite, and a big-time journalist. Quint Jones it is.

Quint's Physiological Dimension

Quint's mother, let's say, was part Native American—her mother was a full-blooded northern Paiute, and he inherited her flashing dark eyes and her copper-colored skin. He has his father's red hair, and he's big and broad shouldered like his father. He has a strong, determined air about him.

Quint has exceptional eyesight. He's ambidextrous to the point that it is a handicap: he can't tell his left from his right and often gets directions screwed up. Sometimes he even makes a mistake and bets out of turn in a poker game, which he tries to prevent by wearing a turquoise-and-silver bracelet on his right wrist.

Quint's Sociological Dimension

Let's say Quint is from Reno, Nevada (fancy that, just where Garret is exiled!). Quint's father, Buster Jones, was a cardsharp, and his mother, Lorna, was a one-time hooker who became a puppeteer. Let's say his father was killed in a casino parking lot after winning twenty thousand dollars in a poker game. Quint and his mother witnessed the killing but could not identify the culprits. This happened when Quint was nine years old.

Quint loved his father. His father used to take him camping on horseback and cross-country skiing. He taught Quint to shoot a gun and how to read "tells," the little movements, tics, and gestures of poker players that give away their hands. Quint has became so good at it that people suspect he's psychic.

His mother, in shock after the murder of her husband, started living a fantasy life, believing her puppets were real, treating them like members of the family.

So Quint's childhood was divided into two parts. At the moment of his father's murder, everything changed. He lost his loving father, and his mother lost touch with reality and became a child-woman.

Quint grew up in the high desert near Reno, in the foothills of the Sierra Nevada mountains on a ranch called Buster's Rancho. Their ranch house was two old mobile homes connected by a crudely made plywood passageway. The ranch covered six acres, and they had exactly one horse as livestock. Quint's mother made puppets as her hobby and sometimes did seamstress work for the showgirls at the clubs in Reno.

As a kid living in the desert, Quint didn't have any playmates, and the hills prevented TV reception, so he read a lot. His mother took him to the library every week, and he took home stacks of books. When he was alive, his father was always either flush and spent money like a drunken sailor or dead broke and spent whatever he could beg or borrow. His father was blustery and outgoing (hence the nickname "Buster"), a big, red-headed, broad-shouldered Irishman, with a flushed-red face and an infectious laugh. Life to him was a lark. He thought of most people as suckers to be fleeced. But he loved his wife and his son, and there was always food on the table and propane in the tank.

His mother's family had been wiped out in a fire that swept her home while she was away at summer camp. She was twelve when it happened, and afterwards she was brought up by a rather cold and cruel aunt who made a marginal living in the change booth at a casino in Elko. Always poor, Quint's mother ran away at sixteen and fell in with a wild crowd and ended up dope addicted and a hooker in Las Vegas. She was twenty-eight and already burnt out when she met Quint's dad, who said he didn't care what her past was—he'd make her his queen. He took her to his ranch, which turned out to be six acres of desert and two aged mobile homes, but she didn't care. She was happy there and beat her drug habit. She loved her husband and her son and her simple life. She put on puppet shows at the local hospitals and nursing homes. Making people happy gave her great joy. Quint loved her deeply. When he was seventeen and she was forty-eight, she died of ovarian cancer.

Quint's education was minimal. He was never a good student even though he was a voracious reader: he was far too much of a daydreamer. He quit school at sixteen to take a job at a stable, where he started playing poker with the ranch hands and soon spent more time gambling than working. He was good even then, but he did get wiped out from time to time—he was often too reckless. He was learning his craft. He was haunted by dreams of his father's death.

Quint loved the desert. Out there, often alone, he felt free. He would go out into the desert with his horse for days and weeks at a time, wandering around. The desert, to him, had great beauty and serenity.

When his mother died, he felt alone in the universe. He hitchhiked around the United States, won and lost money at poker, got beat up a few times, felt a crushing loneliness. He finally joined the navy on a whim and became a machinist on a repair tug in Bremerton, Washington.

He liked the navy. And he liked being a machinist. He liked fooling around with the guys, hanging out in the bars near the base, playing cards, shooting pool. It was an easy life. You do your job, you don't make waves, and you do things not the wrong way or the right way but the navy way, and everything will be all right.

At twenty-one he met and married Lacy Todd, daughter of the owner of the biggest Chevy dealer around.

Lacy saw Quint as a ruggedly handsome, very manly man—a man like her father, though at the time she'd dropped out of college and was rebelling against him. She'd married a sailor instead of the lawyer her mother had picked out for her.

Quint was handsome and seemed shy. A Mel Gibson type. He was dark and mysterious. She had always suspected her father was a bigot, so Quint's Indian blood made him even more desirable. Lacy married him thinking she could make him over into her own image. She'd show his muscles off at the tennis club, dress him up in a new blue blazer, and have his teeth capped.

None of these plans worked out for her.

Quint got out of the navy and took his bride home to Buster's Rancho. By the time their daughter Nevada (later changed to Thayer) was born, the marriage had already gone sour. Lacy grew bored of living in the desert; she wanted a fast life in the big city. Reno, she was fond of saying, was nowhere. They fought, divorced, and she moved to San Francisco, taking six-year-old Nevada with her. She later married Roland Smite, who possessed a lot of very old money.

Quint loves his daughter, Nevada, deeply, but only sees her a few times a year. This, of course, is another wound.

He became very good at playing poker over the next few years, but he never took joy in "taking a sucker" as his father had. He saw poker as a way to make enough money to be free to hunt and fish, roam free in the desert, and "just have time to be yourself" as he liked to put it. He never wanted much. A few acres, a good horse, a few good friends, and family. So far he has not found the right woman.

Quint's Psychological Dimension

Quint has a special talent—he can read people's faces and gestures and know what cards they're holding—and as a result he knows people and can often guess correctly about their inner feelings and motives. He calls this talent his "people radar." With women his radar sometimes goes haywire. Despite his good looks, he's rather uneasy with women. His ruined marriage has left him bitter.

Quint is a good horseman and likes to be out of doors. He drinks heavily at times, especially when he's down or depressed, but he never gets sloppy drunk. He's able to concentrate and, in a big-stakes poker game, has nerves of steel. He'd rather be alone than be with people. He's often moody, but can, when with friends, have a good time. He likes to sing.

Women like him for his gentleness, and men like him because he's a good sport and is a skilled outdoorsman. He does have a temper, though; when people put down Indians (as they often do in the West), he's quick to offer to punch their lights out.

Okay, this will do for a quick sketch of Quint.

Quint's Journal

The following is a journal entry written in Quint's voice:

From the time I was six years old my old man would get out the cards, and I'd play poker with him for my allowance money, and many were the weeks I went without. He taught me that gambling was life itself, and to be good at gambling was to be good at living, and I hold to that. My old man taught me that everything in the world was chance and luck, and poker was the essence of life, knowing what the other fella was thinking, and what he was thinking was painted in neon on his face if you knew how to read it. A slight flush to the cheeks, a nervous tic at the corner of the eye, a narrowing of the pupils. Sometimes it was smell. You could sometimes smell it when a man was bluffing you.

If you don't have a sense of smell, my old man said, you ought not to be cardin' for a livin'.

My old man did get low at times, when he'd be on a losing streak, and then he'd drink; and when he'd drink, he was like another man, sullen, but he never got violent. He only did harm to himself.

I thought back on it later when I was reading this crazy

book by a communist named Bertolt Brecht. He said something like a good man has good luck and a bad man has bad luck, but that's not the way it is. I wish it were like that, but it isn't. Luck just happens—it's like spring rain; it falls on everybody's garden, the good and the bad.

I know it's funny that a guy who never had much schooling like me likes to read, but I do, and I read just about anything. I like books that make me think. I've read all of Friedrich Nietzsche about four times. He makes me think. I don't always agree with him, especially about that superman stuff, but he is a challenge. And maybe I don't understand all that superman stuff, but I will keep trying.

My father was a good Christian, at least he said he was. He taught me you were doing good to teach others not to covet your goods. He said when a man sat down to play poker with you, he was asking to be converted. My old man said Jesus said to give to the poor, and by taking another player's money, you're teaching him Christian charity.

My mother said he was a blasphemer, but she said it with a grin.

People aren't just one way or the other, like most people think. People are like baling wire: you put the pressure on, they bend every which way. The truth be known, I got a few friends, but most people need too much straightening out to be worth the trouble.

When my old man got killed, old Charley Whitebeard, he'd come over and teach me what my old man didn't get around to teaching me. Charley Whitebeard taught me how to hide my hand so they'd never tell what I was holding and how to make 'em think I wasn't bluffing when I was and I was when I wasn't, which, he said, was all there was to the religion of poker. It wasn't knowing, like the song said, when to hold 'em and when to fold 'em, it was a matter of making the other fella believe. Charley Whitebeard was not a Christian; he only believed, he told me, in the god of chance. He died from a hemorrhage when he was eighty-two, holding four cards to a flush and betting five hundred dollars on the come.

My mother was a sweet woman who never scolded me a single time, who hugged me whenever I came in or was going out, who taught me that the simple life was the good life and not to love money—or the things it will buy—too much. She made wonderful puppets—Martians and ghosts and monsters—and did puppet shows for me, making up her own stories and having her puppets act them out on a cardboard-box stage she'd made. It was magical.

But she had no magic for herself. When my old man died, it was like the air had gone out of her lungs.

It's not the money that draws me to the poker table; it's the feeling I get when I lay them cards down and I have three fours and they have three threes. It's an almost mystical feeling I get when there's maybe a grand lying on that table and I have maybe a jack high and they have three kings and I make them fold. It's almost like God is saying I've got the power.

Not that I believe in God. Maybe I do, but my old man taught me that organized Christianity was just another con, and my ma said God was just another kind of make-believe. When I see all the bad things in the world, the hungry kids, people bombing people, I think, how can there be a God who loves people, how could he let this happen? It just never meant anything to me.

Charley Whitebeard says God is the Great Spirit, and Charley says he's mighty pissed at the white man and he's gonna turn all the white people into turds one day. I tell him I'm white and he says I'm enough Indian that I'll be saved, that my soul is Indian. And I don't care about what the white man cares about, his stocks and bonds and a Mercedes automobile. He says I think like an Indian because I love this earth. Maybe I do love this earth, and maybe I feel that there is a Great Spirit who cares about the earth and all his creatures, including us. . . .

Quint, though not a hero, has many heroic qualities so that he will be worthy of the hero.

Please note that the biographies and qualities of the characters are not set in stone at this point. I can add or subtract new facets of character and new elements in my characters' backgrounds, which may occur to me later, that will help make the story more emotionally powerful, more dramatic, even more mythic.

The key thing about the hero-Lover relationship is that they have a major and fundamental difference between then, and yet there is a great pull bringing them together. This is the secret, of course, that accounts for the popularity of romance novels and romantic subplots in novels and films. The two lovers are repelled, yet strongly attracted. It's a kind of inner conflict that brings the reader or viewer so strongly into the story world that the real world goes away. The reader may be drawn into the story with so much force that the fictive dream becomes the reader's reality.

When creating the lovers as a set, you need to think about what it is that will keep the lovers apart as well as together. Sometimes it is family status that keeps them apart. This is one of the things that is going to keep Garret and Quint apart. She's an upper-class Easterner, and he's a lower-class Westerner.

It need not be class; it might be racial. "Ma and Pa would never go along with me marryin' a Paiute" is an example of that kind of thing. *Guess Who's Coming to Dinner* (1967) was an example of this: the white daughter brings home a black man (played brilliantly by Sidney Poitier) she plans to marry, and the liberal parents—Spencer Tracy, in his last film, and Katharine Hepburn—freak. Audiences loved it, and critics puked all over it.

One of my students recently wrote a story in which the daughter of some old hippie radicals from the sixties brings home a space alien she intends to marry—a fresh handling of this theme.

The thing that repels the two lovers may be internal and not just pressure from friends, family, and community. Say there's a great difference in age. A writer I know sold a long short story about a woman who falls in love with a much younger man, which was produced as a made-for-TV movie. Same idea, and it worked well.

When creating the hero and the Lover, make them different in many ways so that there will be conflict between them at many levels. This is the reason you want your characters to be well orchestrated.

Okay, in the present case of Garret and Quint:

- She's a reporter with a career. He's a gambler and works only when there's a big game or a tournament.
- She's a careerist. He's never had a steady job in his life.
- She's high energy. He's laid-back.
- She loves New York. He hates big cities, especially New York.
- She hates Reno, the desert, the West. He loves Reno, the desert, hates the East.
- She's college educated, Ivy League. He's self-educated, no college, didn't finish high school.
- She's never been married, likes kids, but thinks they get in the way of success. He has been married, has a daughter he adores, and would love to have a family.

There must also be qualities about the hero's love that attract. The reader needs to feel this attraction. Naturally, there's physical attraction. But in this case it is something more. For one, they see the heroic qualities in each other. They see each other as self-sacrificing. They see the courage in each other. They see each other as wounded. He has a sixth sense about people that she admires, and a kind of folk wisdom, and so on. She also marvels that he's so well-read. This will not be love at first sight, of course, but it will grow as the story progresses. They're both rather rugged individualists and, to some extent, make their own laws. Neither is a slavish conformist, and that's something they like in each other.

Maybe they will grow to overcome their prejudices. We shall see. Now that we have our hero, Evil One, and Hero's Lover, we'll have a look at other characters we might be meeting along the way.

Other Mythological Characters

On the journey, the hero will encounter other characters who appear over and over again in myth-based stories. We have already discussed the characters usually (but by no means exclusively) found in the world of common day: the Wise One, the Magical Helper, the Armorer, the Herald, the Loved One of the Tearful Good-bye, the Threshold Guardian, and the Hero's Sidekick. We've also discussed the two characters more commonly encountered first in the second part of the journey in the Mythological Woods: the Hero's Lover and the Evil One. Of course there's no rule about these things. You might have the Wise One, say, show up in the woods and have the hero meet the Evil One in the world of the common day. You might have the hero meet the Armorer late in the story or come across the Magical Helper deep in the woods. As I said before, *the myth-based elements need to serve the story you're creating, not the other way around.*

Here are the myth-based characters who usually, but not always, show up first in the Mythological Woods:

The Evil One's Sidekick

The Evil One is like the hero, too, in that he or she has one or more Sidekicks. Remember, the Hero's Sidekicks are slightly less heroic than the hero—they are what I call a "pale imitation"—but the Evil One's Sidekick need not be a pale imitation of the Evil One. The Evil One's Sidekicks may actually be more powerful and more menacing than the Evil One.

The Rival

This character is in love with the Hero's Lover, forcing the hero into competition. Humbert Humbert has a couple of rivals for the love of Lolita, as an example. The Rival is frequently found in romance novels. The Rival is often favored by the hero's family and friends as being more suitable than the Hero's Lover.

The Trickster

This is a great character in the hands of a skilled fiction writer. The Trickster is a practical joker, who can be on the side of the hero or against the hero. Batman's enemies the Joker and the Riddler are incarnations of the Trickster. The thing about a Trickster is that sometimes you don't know which way he or she will go. Is the Trickster with you or against you? The TV program *Cheers* had a wonderful Trickster, Harry, the con man. So have many films, including *The Flim Flam Man* (1967) and *The Sting* (1973).

The Crone

She's a delightful character. She's old and ugly, usually twisted and gnarled. Think of the three Crones Macbeth meets who foretell his future. The Crone may be the Wise One or the Fool as well.

The Fool

The Fool is a character who everyone knows is, well, a fool. Fools often mutter nonsense, sometimes in rhyme, and act crazy. The thing is, the Fool really is not a Fool at all, but no one listens to the Fool and the wisdom he or she has to offer. Often, the only one to wake up and listen to the Fool before it's too late is the hero. That the hero recognizes the inherent wisdom of the Fool is one of the most common and enduring mythological motifs and never fails to please. Sometimes the hero wakes up too late.

Woman-as-Mother

The hero encounters women in many guises. The Woman-as-Mother is a common one. This character is wise, loving, kind, nurturing, forgiving, self-sacrificing. She is Pilar in Hemingway's *For Whom the Bell Tolls* (1940) and Mrs. Cratchit in *A Christmas Carol*.

The Femme Fatale

The Femme Fatale is the female character who lures the male hero to his doom. Circe, the witch who kept Ulysses as her boy toy and turned his men into swine, is such a character. Two hit films, *Black Widow* (1987) and *Fatal Attraction* the same year, used this character as the Evil One. In a sense, Lolita was a Femme Fatale; she certainly lured Humbert Humbert to his doom.

The God with Clay Feet

This character seems godlike in his power. Almost always a male figure, he seems supreme and wise, but in the end turns out to be lacking. Sometimes he's the Evil One. The female hero often falls in love with him. He often serves as the female hero's mentor or even lover. Romance heroines often throw in with this godlike figure who is opposing the hero, but the heroines always wise up in the end when Mr. Clay Feet's true colors begin to show.

The Shape-Shifter

The Shape-Shifter is not actually a character; rather, shape-shifting is an ability almost any character might engage in. Shape-Shifters look one way at one time and another way at another time. Superman is a Shape-Shifter. So are Batman, the Green Hornet, and the woman with multiple personalities in *Three Faces of Eve* (1957). Cinderella is a Shape-Shifter: she goes from being Miss Ugly of the Ashes to a beautiful princess. Hawkeye in *M*A*S*H* (1969) is, in a sense, a Shape-Shifter. As discussed in *How to Write a Damn Good Novel II: Advanced Techniques,* Hawkeye is a "dual character," a Shape-Shifter, switching back and forth between dedicated and gifted surgeon and flamboyant prankster.

Woman-as-Goddess

The Woman-as-Goddess is Helen of Troy. She's perfect. Usually beautiful, but also loving, caring, and sexy. Think of Grace Kelly in *High Noon* (1952), the Good Witch of the

North in *The Wizard of Oz* (1939), Natasha in *War and Peace*.

The Saint

Here we have an innocent, saintly, pious, and world-weary intellectual in *The Petrified Forest* (1936). Prince Mishkin in Dostoyevski's *The Idiot* (1869) is another well-known example. Jean Valjean in *Les Misérables,* as mentioned earlier, is such a character, and so is the bishop in that story. The TV series *Kung Fu* featured Caine, a Buddhist priest of the Sholin temple, as a saintly hero.

The Whore (the Temptress)

She's the worldly woman, in contrast to the goddess, who's almost always a sort of innocent. The Whore is usually a kindly, sympathetic character, but isn't always. She can be nasty at times. The key thing about her is that she's sexually available for a price. Delilah is one, of course. So is Mrs. Ramirez in the film *High Noon* in a very sympathetic portrait of the Woman-as-Whore, as is Belle Watling in *Gone with the Wind.*

The Nymph

A young temptress who may be just a flirt. Lolita was a Nymph. Humbert Humbert called her a "nymphette," but she was, mythologically speaking, a nymph like any other. As mentioned above, the Nymph may be a Femme Fatale as well.

The Woman-as-Bitch

She is very difficult to get along with—complaining, demanding, volatile. Lady Catherine de Bourgh in *Pride and Prejudice* is one; Big Nurse as the Evil One in *One Flew over the Cuckoo's Nest* is another.

There are other characters called stereotypes who no doubt have mythic roots: the lowlife, the drunk, the goof-off, the loudmouth, the ditz, and so on. They are certainly familiar to readers, but they don't seem to have the same resonance as truly mythic characters such as the Evil One or the Trickster, the Femme Fatale, and others.

Casting the Characters

In *The Blue Light*, which of these characters might we meet?

Certainly the Evil One and the Hero's Lover.

Maybe a Fool, a Magical Helper, Woman-as-Goddess, Woman-as-Whore, Woman-as-Bitch, a Trickster, a Shape-Shifter.

When writing with the hero's journey in mind, these are the kinds of questions you should keep asking yourself. If the mythic characters and the mythic motifs fit into the construction of your hero's journey, then use them. If not, leave them out.

If you do use them, you'll need to do the complete biographical workup on them if they're going to be major characters. For a minor character, you'll probably get by with just a short background sketch.

Okay, now that we have our possible cast of characters complete, we're ready for the hero to cross the threshold and enter the Mythological Woods, where we'll meet some of the characters and the initiation of the hero will take place.

6

Fasten Your Seat Belt, the Journey Begins

Over the Threshold and into the Woods

The Mythological Woods in the days of yore might have been a dark and foreboding place full of dragons and monsters, a strange and wondrous place. Ulysses went into the cave of a cyclops. Jason, after the Golden Fleece, went into the Land of Colchis. Even in modern fantasies, the Mythological Woods can be weird. Alice's Wonderland, Oz, all Star Wars planets are all strange places full of fabulous forces.

But unless you're writing a fantasy, horror, or science-fiction novel, the Mythological Woods is not going to be Wonderland or Oz, or even all that strange. But it will be *different* from what the hero has been experiencing in the world of the common day. The important thing about the Mythological Woods is that during the initiation the hero is not in the common-day world. The hero has gone to a place where he or she is a stranger, and to the hero, that place, that Mythological Woods, can be very strange indeed.

As an example, on the *Colombo* TV series, poor raggedy

Colombo in his wrinkled raincoat, driving his beat-up old Peugeot (as if the L.A. police chief would let one of his men drive around in an old junker like that), is sent to investigate a murder in a strange place: a rich guy's mansion, a movie studio, a fashion-modeling business. Colombo is a bowling alley kind of bird. His natural habitat is where truckers and factory workers hang out, not where the rich and famous roam. For him, the Mythological Woods—the strange place full of wonders—is any upper-class joint.

- In *One Flew over the Cuckoo's Nest*, McMurphy is a street tough. He's been sentenced to a county work farm. He's very much a lowlife. For him, the Mythological Woods is an insane asylum, and the monsters he is to confront are members of the psychiatric establishment.
- In *Carrie*, Carrie's world of common day is the loneliness of her room. Then plain and socially inept Carrie is asked to the prom by the most popular boy in school. In fact, she's going to be prom queen. For her, this is indeed a strange and wondrous place for her to be.
- Scrooge, in *A Christmas Carol*, is taken by three ghosts into his own past, present, and future: that is his Mythological Woods.
- Mitch McDeere, in *The Firm*, goes to work in a law firm that is laundering money for the Mob—his Mythological Woods.
- Tolstoy's Anna Karenina goes into the world of illicit love, as do Flaubert's Madame Bovary and many other tragic heroines.

- Pierre Buzuhov, in *War and Peace*, goes into the Mythological Woods of war. He wanders around the battlefield looking for truth—that battlefield is his Mythological Woods.
- The Mythological Woods can be the hero's own hometown, as long as it has become changed somehow. Take as an example that wonderful film *Invasion of the Body Snatchers* (1956). The hero, a doctor, has a problem! His patients are being replaced by soul-less duplicates. He's right at home, yet he's in a Mythological Woods.
- Another example of the hero's hometown as the Mythological Woods is *High Noon* (1952). Because the town, under the threat of gunmen, changes from the town the hero has known and loved, it has become an alien place.

Now That He's in the Woods, the Hero Must Learn the New Rules

The first thing the hero has to do, sensibly, since he's in a strange place, is to learn the new rules. This doesn't mean necessarily that the hero will obey the rules, but they will have to be learned.

A cartoon-type myth-based story—which is certainly not great literature, but is indeed great escapist fiction—is Ian Fleming's *From Russia with Love*. In this story, Bond receives his call to adventure from M, his boss. It seems some female clerk in the Soviet embassy has fallen in love with Bond from afar, and she's written a letter—hence the title,

"From Russia with Love." The letter states that if he'll come to Istanbul, where she works as a cryptographer, she'll help him snatch a *lektor*, a secret decoding device. The lektor is the prize, of course, which Alfred Hitchcock derided as "the McGuffin." The McGuffin is a mythical lion that prowls the hills of Scotland as Big Foot prowls the hills of the Pacific Northwest. Hitchcock, however, defined the McGuffin as the thing the spies cared everything about, but the audience cared nothing about. Anyway, the lektor is the boon that Bond hopes to bring back to his community, even though most readers haven't the slightest idea what a lektor is.

Bond and M both know that there's some kind of a game being played here, which only adds to the attraction of the assignment. Off Bond goes to Istanbul. There he meets Kerim Bey, the local British contract agent, who tells him that the game is played differently here (an ally and Threshold Guardian). For one thing, it's a matter of family and involves not only international espionage but the settling of old scores between ethnic groups and clans within the same ethnic group. Bond is soon fighting Bulgarians and Romanians and Russians on the side of the Gypsies and Turks. It's all a confused mess, but he quickly learns the new rules.

Brody, the sheriff hero in *Jaws*, must learn how to deal with small-town bureaucracy and small-town minds. His Mythological Woods is the same town he's been living in; the difference is that the town is now threatened by a shark. He goes more deeply into the woods, out on the open sea in a boat, which for him is a wondrously strange place.

One of the truly great films of all times is *The African Queen*. It is not only a great example of well-orchestrated lovers; it's a great example of learning the new rules. In case you have not read the book by C. S. Forester or seen the film starring Katharine Hepburn and Humphrey Bogart, I'll synopsize it for you.

Rosie is a churchy, straitlaced spinster out in the African bush helping her brother, the pastor of a local church in German East Africa at the start of World War I. The Germans (the minions of Kaiser Wilhelm, the Evil One) come and burn down the native village. Rosie's brother dies of shock. Rosie goes off on the *African Queen,* a beat-up old thirty-foot river steamer. Her captain is a gin-swilling lowlife, Charley Alnut. When Rosie first gets on the boat, she has to learn the new rules. She has to learn the left side of the boat is the port side and the right side is the starboard side. She has to learn how to steer down the rapids and how to handle the drunken, irascible Charley Alnut, who is operating under the delusion that he, not she, is the captain.

Charley, who is a hero on his own journey (yes, you can have two or even more in the same book), has new rules to learn as well, not the least of which is how to get along with a woman on board, especially one who expects him to take the boat downriver and blow up a German gunboat. Never mind that the river is unnavigable: there's a German fort to pass by; there are alligators and bugs; and the river delta turns into little more than a marsh before it reaches the lake.

But mostly they both have to learn the rules of love, and often this is the most important thing the hero must learn. The love the hero finds frequently hinders rather than helps the hero overcome the Evil One. What falling in love often does, however, is to help the hero heal his or her wound. It's a truly wonderful romantic adventure story. See the film; it has a much more satisfying ending than the novel.

The New Rules in *The Blue Light*

Okay, what are the new rules our hero, Garret, will have to learn? Again we turn to the old brainstorming technique to see whether we can come up with a few possibilities.

- Garret may have to learn to survive in the desert. She's a city gal, remember. The desert itself is a rather harsh and challenging environment full of bugs and snakes and sandstorms.
- Garret may have to learn to deal with the Evil One. She has never before been in a life-and-death struggle.
- Garret will meet Quint on the journey and fall in love. There are always new rules to learn in that game.
- Garret may learn that the facts are less important than the perceived reality—in other words, she's now in the world of the mysterious blue light, where belief is more important than reality.
- Garret will have to learn to trust.

Along the way, there may be more things for Garret to learn. We'll have to see how things develop.

The Hero Is Tested—Sometimes Called the Trail of Trials

As the hero is learning the new rules, he or she will be tested. In dramatic terms, the tests are called "obstacles." A character grows (meaning character development, as your high school English teachers called it) as a result of these tests and in the process of meeting these tests. The small increments of growth in the hero are often thought of as the hero overcoming the limitations in himself or herself, learning new skills, or finding inner resources the hero didn't know he or she had.

The hero does not always pass these tests. In fact, the hero often fails the tests, but grows as a result.

- Pierre Buzuhov, in *War and Peace*, is put against the wall to be shot, then goes on a death march with Napoleon's army through the Russian winter. He's tested. He has a chance to kill Napoleon but cannot bring himself to pull the trigger. He comes to love his fellowman and see that there is purpose in suffering.
- McMurphy, in his war against Big Nurse in *One Flew over the Cuckoo's Nest*, passes some tests—he manages to put some spine into his fellow inmates. Others, he fails. He underestimates Big Nurse and her power, as an example.
- Brody, in *Jaws*, has to overcome his seasickness, deal with the stupid town council, contend with the iras-

cible, shark-fighting Captain Quint, and, of course, duel with a great white shark.

- Mitch McDeere, in *The Firm,* has to contend with conspirators in his firm working for the Mafia, who try to kill him.
- Leamas, in *The Spy Who Came in from the Cold,* pretending to be a turncoat, is severely tested by the communist spies who are holding him.
- In *The Red Badge of Courage,* Henry is tested by combat.
- In *Anna Karenina,* Anna, tested by illicit love, is ostracized from upper-class society and by the wrath of her husband.
- Elizabeth, in *Pride and Prejudice,* is tested by the game of love and the galling pride of Mr. Darcy.

Mythological Motifs

Mythologists call these scenes "functions," which may be slightly confusing because they call members of the mythological cast of characters "functions" as well.

Some motifs we've already discussed, the ones that occur in the world of common day: the Herald bringing the call to adventure; the hero seeking advice from the Wise One; the hero visiting the Armorer; the tearful good-bye with a Loved One; the warning from the Threshold Guardian.

Recurring motifs are found in the Mythological Woods as well. It might be good to meditate on them, to imagine such a scene in your story, and to ask yourself whether your story might be enriched if you had such a scene. Many of them may appear more than once and, of course, may appear in the world of the common day. But, more often than not, they will appear during the initiation or the return.

The Hero Is Rescued by "Divine" Intervention

This motif should not be used more than once in a story. In *The African Queen,* as an example, after the two heroes have taken the boat all the way down the river, it gets beached on a sand bar. All is lost, it seems. It rains. The river rises, and the boat floats out onto the lake, and the heroes are saved. Divine intervention, in a way, proves the hero is beloved by the gods. In ancient myths, the gods often rescued heroes, such as when Zeus sends Hermes to rescue Ulysses by lifting Circe's curse.

The Hero Is Rescued by Allies

This motif should not appear more than once in a story either. Robin Hood, as an example, is condemned to death by Prince John and is rescued by the Merry Men with Maid Marian's help. This proves that the hero is beloved. Leamas is rescued from the cellar where he's being held. Scrooge is rescued from his living hell by the three spirits of Christmas.

The Hero Shows a Willingness to Die for a Cause

Sometimes, the hero not only shows willingness; he or she does die in the service of a cause. El Cid died in service to his cause—then was strapped to his horse even after death to lead his men to victory. McMurphy gives his life. But it is more common for the hero only to show a willingness. Marshal Kane in *High Noon* is an example. In *The African Queen,* there's a wonderful scene where Charley Alnut is facing what looks like certain death and the cause appears doomed. He says, "I'm not sorry I came, not sorry one bit."

The Hero Attends a Celebration

At this celebration, the hero is often the guest of honor—or at least a special guest—but, on the other hand, may come uninvited. Robin Hood goes to Prince John's celebration to declare himself for King Richard and promises to raise an army of the oppressed to fight against Prince John. In *From Russia with Love,* Bond attends a party at the Gypsy camp. *War and Peace* opens with a grand ball. In *My Fair Lady,* there's a ball where Eliza Dolittle charms the prince and is passed off as a duchess, a special guest indeed. *Cinderella* is all about a ball and is one of the most beloved myth-based stories of all times.

The Hero Changes Costume

The change of costume is, of course, emblematic of a change of circumstance or growth in the character. When Lawrence of Arabia, as an example, goes out into the desert to be initiated by the Arabs, he changes costume more than once: first into Arab desert garb, signifying his leaving the world of common day; then into fancy, stunning white Arab garb, when he becomes a leader. Eliza Dolittle changes garb when she first enters the Mythological Woods of Professor Higgins's home; later she dons a fancy dress when she's to be tested on a trip to the racetrack; then she puts on a gown to go to the ball, where she triumphs.

The Hero Faces Natural Fears

They include the terrors of heights, fire, wild animals, creepy things, dark places, claustrophobic spaces, physical combat, inhospitable environments, monsters, evil spirits, and perils involving water: storms at sea, rapids, and so on. The James Bond films exploit these natural fears over and over again. Bond fights on airplane wings, swings from the Golden Gate Bridge, gets tossed into shark tanks. Confronting beasts and other physical dangers is a very ancient mythological motif. It's no secret why it resonates with readers, because every reader on earth shares these fears.

The Hero Has a Change of Consciousness

He or she may enter a drug state, a dream state, or simply get drunk. Sometimes heroes are given knockout drops or are bewitched. Heroes often have visions in dreams. Ulysses gets drunk on Circe's wine and is bewitched. McMurphy gets drunk at the party when he springs the inmates.

The Hero Uses Magic

In the case of modern heroes like Bond, the magical devices are high-tech devices. Often now the hero uses computers in magical ways. One of my students, Cara Black, has created a wonderful detective series from Soho Press; in *Murder in the Marais* (1998) the hero, Aimée Leduc, is a computer expert and has a partner in her business, a dwarf named René, who is a wizard with a computer. He's her Magical Helper.

The Hero Has Magic Used Against Him

In fantasy stories magic is often used against the hero. Morgan le Fay used it against King Arthur. Often in science-fiction stories some modern technical device is causing all the trouble. Think of *War of the Worlds*: what the Martians bring are sort of magical, invincible weapons. The science in *Forbidden Planet* (1956) creates an invisible, all-powerful being that tears people apart. This is magic.

The Hero Falls in Love

Pierre Buzuhov falls in love with the sweet and kind Natasha after his first wife (the Woman-as-Bitch) dies. Anna Karenina falls in love with Vronski, the God with Clay Feet. Michael Corleone falls in love with Kay, then with the Sicilian girl, whom he marries and who is killed.

The Hero Rescues a Captive

This is an often-repeated motif and is very ancient. Jack in "Jack and the Bean Stalk" rescues his fair maid from a tower. Robin Hood gets the money to redeem his king, who is being held for ransom. James Bond often rescues his lover. Ulysses comes home to rescue Penelope from her suitors. Every TV private eye has rescued hundreds of women held hostage.

The Hero Is Betrayed

The hero may be betrayed by a follower, a Sidekick, or even the Lover. Samson is betrayed by Delilah. In *The Body Snatchers*, in one of the most stunning betrayals ever, the hero's love turns into one of the pod people and betrays him. There are times when the betrayal is central to the plot, as in the case of *The Spy Who Came in from the Cold*.

The Hero Is Marked

This may be some sort of maiming, scarring, branding, or tattooing. In ancient myth, Oedipus has his eyes put out. Samson, too, is blinded. Lawrence of Arabia is given a beating with a cane and is left scarred. These marks usually indicate a change in the character.

The Hero Loses an Ally to Death

These motifs are responsible for some of the most moving moments in fiction. The hero's friend dies. The deaths of Obi Wan Kenobi in *Star Wars* and Prince Andre in *War and Peace* are examples of such moments.

The Hero May Die

This motif will be discussed later at length.

The Hero Explains Himself or Herself

This is a common motif in modern myth-based fiction. Some mythologists theorize that this is because of modern man's increased self-awareness and focus on individuality. In this motif, the hero explains why he is the way he is, usually focusing on the wound. This self-explanation almost always comes before the death and rebirth of the hero and often foreshadows the change the hero will go through. Hamlet's "To be or not to be" speech is an example.

There are two very special motifs that go right to the heart of the hero's journey. One is the death and rebirth of the hero, and the other is the confrontation with the Evil One. They usually, but not always, come toward the end of the initiation. For now, we'll look at creating a stepsheet that takes us to the death and rebirth and the confrontation with the Evil One, which will be treated separately in the next chapter; but first we'll take a look at how one uses these motifs and how a hero learns the new rules and is tested.

Our Hero's Stepsheet Continued: Entering the Woods, Learning the New Rules, and Being Tested

A myth-based story does not need to have all the elements of the hero's journey. In fact, as has been pointed out by Joseph Campbell's critics, there is no actual myth ever discovered that perfectly conforms to the monomyth. When creating your own myth-based fiction you should continually ask yourself: Would my story be stronger, more effective, more dramatic, more engaging, more emotional, and more gripping if I included this or that mythological element? Often the answer is yes, but not always. You must exercise reasonable judgment.

Many of the characters and motifs may be left out with no harm done. The order of the events can be changed without real harm as well, and some of the motifs may be repeated—say, the rescue of the hero, or the hero changes consciousness. Even the death and rebirth of the hero may occur more than once.

I've tried, in *The Blue Light*, to conform to the standard monomyth. If you've read other books or articles on the monomyth, you may have noticed that I've jettisoned some of the common terminology—"supreme ordeal," "inmost cave," "belly of the beast," and so on—and instead I use "confrontation with the Evil One," which is what I observe to be actually going on in effective, modern myth-based stories. "Innermost cave" and such terms seem unnecessarily metaphorical and, hence, confusing. Myth-based fiction is an epic battle between the hero and the Evil One, and what's important is not the cave but the confrontation.

This confrontation may or may not be the supreme ordeal. A hero may be lost in a snowstorm, say, then get tossed off a cliff, and later have a sword fight with the Evil One's chief minion—which is the supreme ordeal? If a really strenuous ordeal occurs before the supreme ordeal, should you cut it? Make it less strenuous? Doesn't make sense to me. I feel there's too much of a value judgment in terminology like

"inmost cave" and "supreme ordeal." All the ordeals are supreme at the time the reader reads them; all the caves are
inmost when the hero is entering them.

The structure of the hero's journey is really quite simple.
The hero becomes initiated by learning the new rules, being
tested, having a death and rebirth, and confronting the Evil
One. The hero will often get hold of something valuable
called the prize and bring it back to the community. There
can be wide variation of the general outline, but basically
that's it.

It's critical to remember that the actions grow out of the
motivations, reactions, and emotions of the characters, and
that we're not just dishing up a bunch of mythological elements tossed in helter-skelter to conform to a pattern.

That said, we'll pick up with our hero when last we saw
her, ready to cross the threshold and enter into the Mythological Woods.

The Stepsheet Continues: The Hero's Initiation Begins: Learning the New Rules/Being Tested.

10. Garret heads out into the desert feeling excited;
    this may be the big story she's been hoping for. She
    is in her four-wheel-drive SUV (sport utility ve-
    hicle) with air-conditioning and hardly notices the
    blistering heat. She leaves the paved state route
    (the precise moment she crosses the threshold) and
    follows a road that looks like something on the

map, but finds it is little more than a couple of ruts. Oh well, no problem—as promised in the TV car ads, her SUV zips right along just like on a freeway.

11. It's a few hours later. Garret is a little lost. (She's learning the new rules, being tested.) Things are quite different out here: she's no longer in the familiar world of common day, and she's beginning to feel a bit uneasy—the desert is so . . . so . . . big! And there's nothing but rocks and dirt and dust. She gets out of the car to spread the map on the hood and is astonished at how hot it is. The blue light was spotted in the southeast, so she heads that way.

12. Garret comes to a small oasis. Here she encounters May Jo, a fey young woman hiking under a sun umbrella and carrying a full pack. May Jo (a mythological character, the Fool) believes superior beings are about to land to bring us an age of peace and happiness. Garret wants to know how she got way out here alone. She says she walked, which is a bit hard to believe. Garret takes May Jo along with her.

13. Garret and May Jo enter a tiny town. It's a ghost town, except for a gas station and a small grocery store, and guess who's there. Right. Quint (the Hero's Lover). He's there going camping with his daughter, Thayer (Woman-as-Bitch); they've ridden in on horseback.

At first Garret finds Quint curiously attractive, despite the fact that she usually finds the Marlboro

Man look a turnoff. Maybe it's the striking combination of red hair and the searching, intense, dark eyes. She senses his inner strength and likes his cocksure attitude. He thinks the blue light is a practical joke; his daughter thinks it's "bunk"—everything is bunk to her. She hates everything but the new horse her father just gave her.

Let's pause here for a moment. This is an important scene in the book, the meeting of the hero and the Hero's Lover. Since I have already drawn the character of Quint in his biography, it might be instructive to see what he'll look like on the page and see how Garret relates to him when she first meets him. He must be both attracted to her and, like most Hero's Lovers, be an antagonist right up until the end.

I don't know the chapter breaks yet, so let's take a guess and say the hero meets the Hero's Lover in chapter 4.

THE BLUE LIGHT

Chapter 4

Garret gripped the wheel tightly as her Pathfinder bounced over the ruts in the road. She glanced over at May Jo, who kept humming to herself, holding her knees, and staring out the window—at what? It seemed to Garret nothing but sand and rock and distant mountains shimmering in the heat. Her air conditioner konked out. God, how she longed for a dip in a cold pool. Her mouth felt like chalk.

They came bouncing over a small rise, and a town

rose up out of the gray sands of the desert before them. A dozen dilapidated buildings, all boarded up, and a gas station/convenience store that looked as if it might still be in business.

"Welcome to Jackrabbit Flats," Garret said.

"The Lord works in mysterious ways," May Jo said.

"Indeed He does."

Garret stopped the Pathfinder at the rusted pumps in front of the gas station. An old man sat in a rocker under a beach umbrella wearing bib overalls and a faded plaid shirt with holes in the elbows. He smiled at them and got up out of his chair and came around to the driver's side. Garret opened her window and was hit with a blast of hot air.

"Ain't got no gas, ma'am. The road don't support no gas truck since they closed the potash plant up on Miller's Butte."

"Should have figured." She shut off the engine. She still had three-quarters of a tank of gas, so she wasn't worried. She could go four hundred miles on that.

Gray dust settled on the Pathfinder from the cloud that had formed behind them when they stopped. She got out and stretched.

May Jo was already out of the car, splashing water on herself from what looked like an old concrete horse trough at the front of the store.

"Got any coffee?" Garret asked the old man.

"Right inside. You'll be wanting to drink some water— the spring over there don't taste too good, but it ain't killed man nor beast yet."

She turned and started into the building. The air felt like a blow-dryer on her face. Across the dirt street was a grove of trees with a sprinkler going. A man and a young woman were watering a couple of horses, brushing them off. He was helping her take the saddle off a horse, obviously trying to please her. She looked way too young for him.

Garret went inside the store. The wooden floor creaked. A ceiling fan rattled. The store shelves were mostly empty: a few cans of beans, a few boxes of oatmeal, some soap. A few shirts and pants. A locked glass case held a few boxes of ammunition. On a hot plate nearby was a galvanized steel coffeepot. She poured herself a cup and tasted it. It tasted burnt and strong and had bitter chicory in it.

The old man grinned. "The way we like it here."

"I'll recommend it to my friends."

"Fifty cents," the old man said.

She put two quarters on the counter.

"You seen this blue light everybody's been talking about?" she asked.

He nodded. "Yup."

"Where exactly was it coming from?"

"Can't rightly say. South, near Lark Ridge, seems like. The first time. Seen it again north of there, maybe twenty-five miles."

"Any idea what's causing it?"

"Yup." he said.

"What?"

"The little people."

"What little people?"

"Leprechauns."

He laughed hoarsely, ringing up the fifty cents on a hand-cranked cash register.

Garret went outside and crossed the dusty street to the shade under two scrawny trees by the sprinkler. The man was sitting propped up against a stone wall reading a book. He was a good six feet and broad shouldered, somewhere around thirty-three or -four, handsome, copper-complected, with flashing, dark eyes.

She felt oddly drawn to those eyes. They were intense, yet not at all unfriendly. They were warm eyes. He looked up at her and smiled an easy smile, and she had the impression that here was a man content with himself.

Garret could see that, under the cowboy hat he was wearing, he had red hair that seemed not to go with the rest of him. He was part Spanish, she thought, or Mexican. Maybe with a little Indian mixed in. Western people liked to claim Indian ancestry—she didn't know why. Maybe to soothe their conscience about taking the Indians' land. The man was dressed like these Westerners always dressed, in jeans, cowboy boots, flannel shirt, silver buckle on the belt. He had a turquoise-and-silver bracelet on his right wrist, looked Navajo. Right out of the nineteenth century. She squinted to see what he was reading—she was sure it was some horse-opera Western, probably ten of them in one thick volume. Then he turned the page, and she could see the cover. Proust, *Remembrance of Things Past.* She gulped—she couldn't believe it.

He glanced up from his book. "Come searching for the light?"

She nodded. "You?"

He shook his head. "On the way to the high country, do some camping. We're waiting out the heat of the day.

Weatherman said it'd be in the midnineties, but he sure blew it on that. I like it hot, but too much heat is no good for the animals."

"Including human animals. Is that really *Remembrance of Things Past* you're reading?"

"I'm wrassling with it. I kind of like it now that I'm into it. It's slow, but it grows on you; it's like a real slow symphony. It's about time and how it sort of slips away and what you have left are these precious shadows called memories. The people really feel things and see things and think things so different from the people I know. Right now I'm on the 'Swan in Love' part. Wish I could read French; I'll bet it's beautiful writing. Even in translation, it's beautiful. Some say Proust is the French Shakespeare—my name's Quint Jones, by the way. That's my daughter, Thayer."

Oddly, Garret was relieved to find out the young woman was his daughter. She didn't think much of cradle robbers. She could see now the young woman was really only a girl. She was brushing her horse in the shade of a dilapidated building, singing to herself.

"I'm Garret Holland," Garret said.

"The reporter?"

"The same."

"Very glad to make your acquaintance. Loved that thing in the paper you wrote about the maid who raised you."

"Thank you so much. I wrote that when I was an undergrad at Yale."

"Liked it so much I clipped it and mailed it to my daughter. She lives with her mother in San Francisco."

"I am so pleased to hear it."

She was also pleased he had an *ex*-wife.

Garret knelt by a pool and splashed some water on her face. The water tasted alkaline. It was warm.

"Anything else of mine you like?"

"Nothing in particular."

"I'm just always so pleased to meet a fan."

"Didn't exactly say that. I said I like the thing about the maid."

"That's it? How about the hard-hitting stuff on the pay-offs for the gambling licenses?"

"That was when you first came to town. I'm not so happy with the stuff you've been doing lately," he said.

"Oh?" Garret felt a twinge of anger rising in her neck. She didn't like critics much. But she said, "If you have a complaint about my work, I'd like to hear it."

"Seems like you're not always straight from the shoulder like a reporter ought to be." He said it with a smile, but she could tell he was serious.

"Well, there's a reason for that."

"I'd like to hear it. I think newspapers are important— the poor man's college, my old man called them."

"Well, it's just that we're competing against television and film; we've got to breathe some life into our stories or we'll be just lining bird cages, and there are not a hell of a lot of bird cages in Reno to line."

"I can see your fears, but truth shouldn't need any help. . . ."

Just then they heard the sound of an approaching vehicle, a loud roar and the grinding of gears.

Okay, that's our Hero's Lover, Quint. I think he'll do nicely. Let's get on with their story.

The Blue Light Stepsheet Continued

14. An old school bus made into a camper rolls into town with a man and his wife and their six brats. They spend their lives chasing UFOs. Garret cleverly wheedles an eyewitness account out of them of a spaceship causing the blue light. The man's account is 99 percent imagination, but it's colorful. Quint is amused. Garret tells him, hey, it's the new millennium, where the news is an entertainment medium. She didn't invent the game; she's just a star player. Garret radios her story to her paper that "eyewitnesses confirm the blue light is definitely emanating from an aircraft, quote, 'unlike any ever seen on earth. . . .' "

15. Quint warns Garret against going into the desert any farther (another Threshold Guardian), and she tells him she doesn't need him to baby-sit her. Then, showing real concern, he tells her to stay on the road, such as it is—at least promise him that. She says thanks, she will. He offers her his handgun to take along, which she declines. She quotes the statistic that more people are hurt with their own guns than are saved.

16. Garret and May Jo are lost in a maze of canyons; attempting to turn around, they get stuck and smash the oil pan. It's blistering hot. The radio is

blocked by the surrounding hills. They will have to hoof it. Garret is certain the way back is due west, but May Jo wants to go on to the "source," as she calls it, south and east. Garret turns around and she's gone. Worried that a fool like May Jo might die out there alone, Garret goes after her on foot (the hero sacrificing himself for another). Trudge, trudge, she goes, through the desert.

17. The sun has set. Garret searches, shining a flashlight, calling May Jo's name. It's cold, windy. She's all twisted around, has no idea where the hell she is. The blue light suddenly appears just as Garret catches up to May Jo, who quickly falls into a trance. The light seems to be undulating, and all around it are twinkling white lights like fireflies. Garret tries to figure where it might be coming from. She takes a sighting (as she did when sailing as a kid with her dad) and marks it, then moves off a few hundred yards and marks another, then again another. The light shuts off abruptly. A few minutes later what looks like car lights come on for a second or two, then shut off. Garret listens—she thinks she hears a motor. May Jo snaps out of her trance and says, "They want us to prepare for the Coming." "Sure," Garret says. "But first we've got to find a phone and get the auto club out here."

18. Garret and May Jo wander around most of the night. Garret gets cold, sprains her ankle, and can't find her SUV (more tests and she's flunking). At three in the morning they finally find the SUV, crawl into sleeping bags, and konk out.

19. The next morning. It's hot and getting hotter. Garret and May Jo trudge along through sand dunes and dry creek beds. Garret finally finds a landmark; the compass is holding steady at last. Then, a miracle! Someone's coming! *(The hero gets rescued.)* Morgan Thorn *(the hero encounters the Evil One)* drives up in his Jeep. Morgan turns on the charm, and our hero is quite taken by his courtly, Boston, upper-crust manners. This is *the first meeting with the Evil One,* but we don't know yet that he's evil. He takes Garret back to her SUV and makes a temporary patch on her oil pan with his extensive tool kit. He's prepared when he goes into the desert. They have a little cookout under a canopy, some chilled white wine—Morgan travels in style. He thinks this blue light is some public-relations gimmick. The blue light will attract people who will damage the fragile ecology, so anything he can do to help her find the real source of the light, he'd be glad to do. Garret likes this man enormously. He's not only the Evil One, he's the God with Clay Feet.

20. Once they get moving, Morgan follows her in his vehicle to make sure hers holds up. Strangely, May Jo rides with him. He's told Garret about an encampment of UFO nuts, and she wants to get some interviews, so they head in that direction.

21. Garret, May Jo, and Morgan Thorn arrive at the UFO-ers encampment. Quint and Thayer are there. It quickly becomes obvious that Quint and Morgan do not like each other. Morgan says good-

bye to Garret, telling her that Quint once lost some money to him in a poker game and is a sore loser. Garret doesn't quite believe it—Quint just doesn't strike her as a poor loser—but when she asks him about it, he refuses to talk about it, saying it's a private matter.

Garret sees, from the dozens arriving hourly, that she's got a lot to do. She interviews some of them and is amazed by what they think are the wonders of the light: it's healing people and so on. She gets a lot of great copy, some of it quite fanciful. Garret finds some religious people who think this is definitely the Second Coming; others think that the blue light is from the future; still others, that it's from another dimension. She's ecstatic. She radios in her report. Her editor, Marion Weibel, thinks it's great and she should get more like it, then warns her that there're a gaggle of reporters coming her way—including the national TV media—and if she intends to scoop them, she'd better hustle.

22. That night the blue light again appears in the sky. Garret gets some great photographs and some great copy. Quint and Thayer and a boy Thayer has just met named Jason are nearby. The blue light has an incredible effect on Thayer: she goes into a sort of ecstasy and passes out. When she comes to, she talks about seeing a beautiful woman who said she would bring light into the world, a new way of knowing. She wants to go out into the desert to touch it. Garret is getting down every

word. Quint says that in the morning they're going back home.

Quint tries to convince Garret that it would be bad for him with his ex-wife if this was in the newspaper. Garret says she has to report what she sees as news.

23. As she lies in her sleeping bag that night, she can't get Quint out of her mind (she's being tested by her strong feelings of attraction). She knows she can't possibly be attracted to him; he's just not her type, he's so . . . so cowboyish, and he's too . . . outdoorsy. She concludes that she feels sorry for him, having such a difficult daughter.

24. In the morning, Garret goes to Quint to tell him she's had a change of heart—she'll write her copy in such a way that no one will be able to figure out it's Thayer—but finds the point is now of little consequence, since Quint has just discovered that Thayer is gone. She and Jason have taken Quint's horses and moved off in the direction of the blue light. Quint borrows Garret's radio and puts a call in to the sheriff, who refuses to mount a search— they're busy hunting for a mess of other kids lost earlier. Besides, Thayer will be OK, the sheriff says; she has blankets, water, etc. They should call back if she doesn't return. Quint says he's going after them—into Hogan's Maze, the very heart of the Mythological Woods, the strangest and most dangerous part. Quint rents an old Jeep from one of the people, but Garret has bought up all the available gas, so she's going along—over his objections.

25. The horses' tracks lead up a narrow valley—too narrow for the Jeep. Quint is forced to go around the mountain. He is confident his daughter has the skills to take care of herself, and he is more worried about Jason. As they go, Quint gives some pointers on surviving in the desert: how to find shade and water seeps in the rocks; what kind of cactus you can squeeze water out of; how to avoid rattlesnakes, biting red ants, tarantulas, and scorpions. He tells Garret of the beauty he sees, the majesty of it, how one can be free there to truly be yourself. She says, to herself, "It's just a hell."

Quint offers to take her into the beautiful high country of the Sierra Nevada on horseback. She's surprised to find how delightful this sounds, but no, she's a city girl. He stops and says that before he keeps pursuing her, he'd like to find out something. Would she mind if he kissed her, just once, as a test? She lets him kiss her. It scares her that she likes it so much. A damn cowboy! He asks to do it again; she says no.

26. A dust storm is coming. Quint shelters the Jeep and goes up a nearby hill to take a look for his daughter and her friend. Garret thinks she sees something not far away that might have to do with the blue light and heads for it. The dust storm envelops her. She's about to have her death and rebirth and then her confrontation with the Evil One.

Before we can go on with this stepsheet, we need to discuss these motifs, which are the subjects of the next chapter.

A Special Note About the Drama

You will notice that the dramatic principles discussed in the *Damn Good Novel* books have been adhered to. There are plenty of story questions raised: What is the blue light all about? Will the two missing kids be all right? What will come of the developing relationship between Garret and Quint? There is conflict between Garret and Quint; there's conflict with the environment; there's conflict between Quint and his daughter, between Quint and Morgan Thorn, and so on. There is conflict, conflict, conflict in every step.

There is also inner conflict in Garret over her feeling for Quint, and there are a lot of emotions to be exploited. There is also incremental emotional growth in Garret, especially in her feelings toward Quint, and her changing feelings toward the desert, all to come.

7

Death, Rebirth, and the Confrontation with the Evil One

The Hero Comes Back from the Dead

The hero's death and rebirth are a powerful motif, perhaps the most powerful and important event on the path the hero travels. In this motif, the hero "dies" in the sense that he or she will no longer be the same person; during the death and rebirth something about the hero's character changes forevermore.

Often the death and rebirth dramatically affect the character's image of self and the way the hero is seen by others. It can be, and often is, the most dramatic moment in the story. In this moment, the coward, say, may be reborn as a hero; a traitor might be reborn a patriot; a timid lover may suddenly propose matrimony; a boy might be reborn a man. Readers and film viewers often cheer at the moment of rebirth. We, as readers, celebrate these death-and-rebirth scenes with our heroes, and in doing so we celebrate the possibilities of human growth and change.

The purpose of the death-and-rebirth motif is to bring

the hero to a new state of consciousness, even a new state of being. Sometimes the death and rebirth are extremely quick, and the change in the character's state of being is vast, such as in *Star Wars,* when Obi Wan Kenobi, a human mentor, Christlike figure, is killed by Darth Vader and is reborn as a spirit.

It need not be as sudden, nor the change quite that great.

The death and rebirth instead may be but emblematic of the changes that have already happened in the hero. When Scrooge throws himself down on the tombstone and rises up in his symbolic death and rebirth, he is already significantly changed by the tests and trials he has been given.

The usual pattern during the hero's initiation after the hero enters the Mythological Woods is this: First, the hero learns the new rules; some he or she obeys, some not. While learning the new rules, the hero is tested and gradually changes, overcoming limitations within, learning new skills, and discovering previously unknown aspects of his or her character.

The tests often are provided by the machinations of the Evil One, but may also be provided by physical challenges, other characters, and inner struggles. Having been changed somewhat, the hero is ready to experience a death and rebirth, which are often a total transformation or the symbolic representation of a total transformation.

That is the usual pattern; it is not the only pattern.

The death-and-rebirth-of-the-hero motif may happen anywhere on the journey: in the world of common day, during the initiation, or on the return. It is not a step in the fixed line of motifs like ducks in a shooting gallery. Myth-based fiction is not cookie-cutter fiction. There is no magic mythic formula; the pattern is infinitely variable. The hero can have not just a thousand faces, but thousands and thousands of faces, and the journey may be in an infinite number of configurations.

So even though the death and rebirth may happen anywhere on the journey, they usually happen during the initiation just before or just after the confrontation with the Evil One.

It is even possible for the hero to have more than one death-and-rebirth experience. It's rare, but it's possible. Or there might be none at all, as in *My Fair Lady*.

- In *The African Queen*, the heroes are washed up on the beach, and it looks as if they're going to die. Exhausted, dispirited, they lie down to await the inevitable. Then they're saved by the rain (God has intervened on their behalf). This is a death-and-rebirth experience. Afterward, they go out on the lake and soak up the feeling of being alive (a change of consciousness) and make plans to sink the *Louisa* (the confrontation with the Evil One). Before they go, they get the boat all spiffed up and get themselves tidied up (a change of costume).

- In *High Noon*, after the marshal has exhausted every avenue for getting help, he must face the Evil One and the Evil One's three henchmen alone. He sits down and writes his last will and testament. This is a symbolic death and rebirth. He is facing up to his own mortality. He then gets up and arms himself, preparing for the confrontation with the Evil One, and goes out into the street to face certain death.

Before this death and rebirth he has been desperately trying to get the townspeople to help him—now he knows he's on his own. He is now a warrior, with a change of consciousness. After he wins the battle, he shows his disgust for the town he once loved to serve by throwing his badge down in the dust.

- Pierre Buzuhov, in *War and Peace,* is taken to the wall to be shot—and just as the firing squad is about to shoot, the festivities are called off. This is a death and rebirth. He started out as a selfish, spoiled, rich boor, and now becomes a human being, full of love and compassion for his fellowmen, and even finds his faith in God.

- McMurphy, in *One Flew over the Cuckoo's Nest,* is first lobotomized (maimed), and then mercy killed by his fellow patients. This is an actual death from which there is no rebirth in a physical sense for McMurphy. The rebirth comes when his spirit comes alive in the Chief, who then smashes his way out of the cuckoo's nest.

- Scrooge has a death and rebirth when the Spirit of Christmas-yet-to-come shows him his own death. His rebirth follows when he awakes to throw open the shutters on Christmas morning, a new man with a new consciousness. He then gets spiffed up to go out and meet the world anew in a change of costume.

- Huck Finn is reported dead and attends his own funeral dressed as a girl. Then he finds that his new friend, Jim, the slave he's been hiding out, has been accused of his murder. He has a complete transformation and helps an escaped slave go north.

- In *Diamonds Are Forever* (1955), James Bond is knocked out and put into a coffin, which is then slipped into a cremation chamber. As the flames lick at the coffin and he struggles to get out, he is rescued. This is a misuse of the death-and-birth motif because, after going through the death and birth, Bond's character is unchanged.

- In the story of Samson and Delilah in the Bible, there is one of the most dramatic and powerful death-and-rebirth motifs ever used. Samson has been blessed by God. He's been given superhuman strength (his special talent), which will only work if he keeps his hair long—a symbol of his dedication to God (the hero marked). First, he heroically slays a bunch of the enemy, the Philistines, with the jawbone of an ass. The Philistine king, the Evil One, sends Delilah, a courtesan, to seduce Samson into giving up the secret of his great power. Samson has a lot of—you guessed it—hubris. In other words, he's pretty stuck on himself, so he gives in pretty easily to Delilah, who wheedles the secret out of him. A minion of the Evil One cuts his hair, and Samson becomes as weak as any man. The Evil One, true to a promise to Delilah, does not shed any of Samson's blood, but he does have him blinded with a hot iron and cast into a pit, where he turns a millstone while his enemies jeer him and lash him and degrade him. But Samson has a rebirth and a change of consciousness. His hair grows back, a change of costume of sorts, and God listens to his prayers. God gives him back his strength; and when the Philistines bring him to their temple to make a public spectacle of him, Delilah helps him to the main pillars, and he brings down tons of rock on the Evil One and all his followers. It's wonderful.

- In Mario Puzo's *The Godfather*, Don Corleone is shot in an assassination attempt and is near death. A war ensues. His son, Sonny, is killed. When the Godfather (Corleone) regains his health (a rebirth), he makes a peace with the other Mafia families and then, having a change in consciousness, passes the reins of power to Michael, his youngest son, who has a death-and-rebirth experience of his own. He shoots "the Turk" and a crooked police lieutenant and has to go into hiding. There he marries the Woman-as-Goddess, who is killed by a car bomb planted by his enemies to kill him. He's had a complete change of consciousness: he's now a ruthless crime lord who has the family's enemies slaughtered all in one day.

- In *Carrie*, Carrie is drenched with pig blood, a baptism of sorts, an ancient symbol of rebirth. Before that moment she believed the lies of the Evil One and God with Clay Feet and thought she really was the prom queen. But in that one second she is reborn—no longer the shy, socially retarded, but psychic Carrie, she is now the terrible angel of doom, a sudden and vast change of consciousness indeed.

- Scarlett O'Hara has a wonderful death and rebirth in *Gone with the Wind*, which is symbolic of the death and rebirth of the South following the War Between the States. Leaving a burning Atlanta, she takes her rival Melanie and Melanie's baby (a self-sacrificing, heroic act) and returns to her home, Tara, only to find the plantation destroyed, her mother dead, and her father out of his mind. She seeks refuge at her neighbors' plantation, Twelve Oaks, only to find it, too, destroyed. Groveling in the dirt for a radish—she's starving—she makes up her mind she'll never go hungry again. At this moment, she throws off the personality of a social butterfly in a striking change of consciousness and sets her mind to rebuilding Tara as a dynamic entrepreneur.

The hero's change may not always be in the direction of making the hero a better human being. In *Lawrence of Arabia*, Lawrence's growth is toward being a more powerful leader until his hubris takes him into an enemy town, where he is jailed, sodomized, beaten, and tossed into the gutter. This is a symbolic death. His Sidekick (played by Omar Sharif) takes him to a cave and heals him. Lawrence is a totally changed man. Now he no longer takes prisoners in battle. He surrounds himself with assassins. He's become a savage brute. It's a rebirth and a vast change of consciousness, but Lawrence has become a monster. The same happens to Dobbs, the hero of B. Traven's *The Treasure of the Sierra Madre* (1935), played in the film version by Humphrey Bogart (1948).

To recapitulate: The death and rebirth can be an actual death and rebirth, as in the case of Obi Wan Kenobi in *Star Wars*. It can be a near-death (severely wounded) and a gradual rebirth with a different consciousness, as in Lawrence of Arabia. Or it can be an almost instantaneous personality switch, as in *Carrie*. It can also be almost completely symbolic, as in *Gone with the Wind*. In the death and rebirth—except in the case of the James Bond–type adventure story—the character has a dramatic change in consciousness.

Back to *The Blue Light* Stepsheet

When last we left her, Garret had wandered off as a dust storm was coming, as you might recall. She has learned the new rules and been tested; now it's time for her to die and be reborn into a new consciousness.

27. The storm hits with a terrible yowl. Though she's only a few yards from the Jeep, Garret quickly becomes disoriented and can't find her way back. She manages to locate a small cave and crawls in. She feels something crawling on her skin—it's a scorpion, and she's been stung! She rushes from the cave back into the storm, in panic and madness—right into the arms of Quint, who's been looking for her. He has a tarp and shelters her. The only reason he found her was that he got confused about which was right and which was left (he has that problem, remember) and he went the wrong way, so he takes no credit.

28. Garret has a terrible reaction to the scorpion bite and starts hallucinating. She sees a beautiful Woman-as-Goddess in the blue light who says, "The eagle will show you the way."

29. When she awakes (the rebirth), Garret discovers an entire day has passed. Quint has set up a camp

in the shade of an overhanging rock and is nursing her. She feels more strongly attracted to him than ever and is grateful that he risked his life for her.

30. Quint goes off for a while. He knows his daughter and Jason have found water and are all right. There are plenty of caves for them to find shelter from the heat that Thayer would know about from her past trips to the area. That night Quint and Garret watch the blue light. She sees it differently (since she's been reborn): it's now very beautiful and gives her a warm, glowing feeling. The desert seems to glow; she sees it differently as well. Now that she's restored to health, they make love.

A Look at the Story

Let's pause in the stepsheet for a moment to see a sample of what our hero is like following this change. We'll start with her waking up from a nap, feeling much better. Quint has gone to search for his daughter and is expected back at any moment. Okay, here's Garret after she's gone through her death and rebirth.

THE BLUE LIGHT

Chapter 16 (just a guess)

Garret awoke as the sun was setting over Pine Tree Butte to the south. She stretched and yawned, and felt great all over. Great just to be alive. She was still a little weak, but she was hungry now and a little stiff from sleeping with a rock poking through the air mattress, but what the hell.

She sat up. She was on top of her sleeping bag, lying next to the Jeep, a green tarp stretched above her like a lean-to. Nearby was a canteen. She gulped some water from it. The water tasted sweet and cool.

She found herself smiling.

There was only one word for the feeling she was feeling, she thought: giddy. She was giddy as a schoolgirl. She noticed her ears were ringing, but the sound was soft, almost melodic. "The music of the spheres" came to mind. She felt in tune with the universe—yes, that was exactly it. It felt strange and wonderful, and she never wanted the feeling to end.

She looked out on the golden, fading sunlight shining on the red rock of the butte. It made the rock glow and shimmer, looking almost magical. The sky was still azure blue, with high, puffy, white clouds lined with pink striping the arching canopy above her. A cool breeze was blowing now. It was as if she were seeing the desert for the first time. Like walking down Broadway at theater time for the first time. The desert was indeed beautiful, and so enormous and expansive, it did make you feel free, just as Quint had said. It cleared the mind and put you in touch with the cosmos.

She heard footsteps and turned to see Quint approaching, his binoculars dangling from around his neck.

"Did you sleep?" he asked.

"I did."

"Feeling better?"

"Ready to wrestle tigers. Soon as I have something to eat."

"Your appetite is back; that's a good omen."

"Any sign of Thayer?"

"She's about twelve miles south of us and is okay."

"How do you know?"

"She sent up smoke signals. I taught her to do that when she was a child."

Garret laughed. "I feel I'm in a time warp."

"The desert is timeless. Modern man has not tamed it, does not really even possess it—maybe that's one reason I love her. Rest some more; drink some water. I'll rustle up some hobo stew."

As he started building a fire, she sipped water.

"I'm beginning to understand," she said. "The desert, it does have its appeal."

"It takes time to grow on you," he said. "Like the French impressionists. Monet, Manet, Degas, Cézanne, Renoir, Van Gogh, Seurat, Gauguin. When I first saw them, I thought, what drivel. It was as if my eyes were seeing light in a new way and they couldn't focus. But I studied them for a week at a show at the Museum of Modern Art in San Francisco—the guards were starting to think I was casing the joint—and now they're my favorite painters. Well, there are some old Dutch masters of light I really like, and El Greco and Raphael, too, when he's not being too sentimental."

"You really are an odd person: a gambler, desert rat, cowboy, art connoisseur."

"Hardly a connoisseur. I just think there are great things in this world, some made by God, some made by man, and you're a fool if you don't learn to appreciate them. To go through your life with your senses dulled would be to miss the trip."

He opened cans and stirred the contents into a large iron skillet. She didn't have to ask: hobo stew was apparently a concoction made of whatever was available.

They sat on a flat rock and ate the concoction with hunks of hard-crusted, slightly stale Italian bread and drank warm beer. Garret ate hungrily, and thought it tasted better than any meal she'd ever had, even in the finest restaurants in Manhattan that came with a bill that would buy you a trip to Europe.

After they cleaned up the dishes, they climbed a small hill nearby, and Quint laid out a blanket, and they sat on it. She was feeling stronger now that she'd eaten.

She took his hand. It was callused and rough, and the fingers were thick and strong.

Then it struck her. She was falling not only for the desert—she was falling for Quint. For a moment she felt frightened, then a little dizzy. This was impossible—he was the goddamn Marlboro Man. Okay, one who liked Monet. But he was still a cowboy, a gambler. It was simply idiotic for her to feel this insane infatuation. It must be because he saved her. Freudian transference. She'd get over it, come to her senses.

Then suddenly he turned to her and kissed her, and she felt the universe spin around her. She felt the old fear, but it quickly fell away. A no came to her lips, but she didn't say it as he kissed her again.

The ringing in her ears was loud now, drowning out her thoughts.

She opened her eyes. She was lying on the blanket looking up at him.

"I still love my ex-wife," he said, "even though she's not loved me for some time. Even though she took my daughter away. I just wanted you to know; I don't take love lightly."

Uh-oh, she thought. *The feeling is mutual. What would Freud say about this?*

He turned away from her now. She sat up and took his hand again. "Isn't it strange," she said, "that in the city I live in the future and in the past, but here I want to live only in the now. Even though part of me knows it's a little foolish."

"More than a little foolish. It's crazy," he said. "I'm usually smarter than this."

"Can't we just live in the now, just for tonight?"

She started to kiss him, and just then she saw a nearby rock turning color, first pinkish and then . . . blue-green.

"Look!" Quint said, pointing behind them.

She turned and there, to the southeast, the blue light stood like a pillar in the night sky. It seemed to hover above the ground, and in it was a cascade of lighter blues and blue-green, and for a moment she thought she saw the woman she'd seen in her dream.

This time she didn't try to find its source. This time she stared at it and felt its effect. Yes, she could see how people would think it was from heaven; it was mysterious and beautiful and pulsing with a life of its own. She stared at it and let herself fall into a sort of reverie, and in the light she could see her life before her, sailing on Long Island Sound with her father, dancing the night away at a resort in Cuba, making mad love with her quarterback boyfriend at Yale in the laundry room of her sorority house in the middle of the night.

And suddenly it was gone. The stars shone above them.

She blinked.

He put his arm around her shoulder.

She kissed him. "For us," she said, "there is now. Let's not think of tomorrow." And she kissed him again, and they lay back down on the blanket, and the stars shown brightly above them.

"Yes," she heard herself saying. "Yes, yes, yes. . . ."

Okay, I think you get the point. The death and rebirth have changed her consciousness and have allowed her to accept love and to see things in a new way.

The Stepsheet Continued

31. In the morning, Garret wakes up to find herself in love, and she's scared. She reverts to her old behavior patterns. She tells Quint how impossible it is, and he says he feels sorry for her because she's so trapped in her boxes.

32. They pick up Thayer's trail and head south. There's somebody following them, so they circle around but can't find whoever it is, only vehicle tracks. A little farther on they find more tracks, then a canyon that isn't on the map. There's a lot of activity here, but what kind? Quint and Garret do not have a clue.

33. They make camp for the night. Garret goes out into the desert to answer nature's call and comes back to find two guys beating up on Quint. He tells her to run, and she does, eluding her pursuer.

34. Garret swings back and follows the tracks of the two men and Quint to a mine. There are a large house and some other buildings. Garret watches and spots Morgan Thorn as he arrives and goes into a building. By the way the others treat him, she knows this is his mine, and she knows they must be up to something illegal.

Okay, in the next scene Garret will prepare herself and then have the confrontation with the Evil One. Before we can continue with the stepsheet, we'll need to discuss this important motif.

Confronting the Evil One: The Usual Pattern, in Brief

The hero has a death and rebirth; then there's a scene where the hero prepares for the confrontation with the Evil One.

Next there's the confrontation, usually in the "lair" of the Evil One.

Sometimes the hero dies, inspiring others to take up the cause.

Sometimes the hero loses and is beaten or jailed or narrowly escapes.

More often, the hero confounds the Evil One, wins a victory, and takes possession of a "prize." The hero will then recross the threshold and return to the community.

Sometimes the "return" section is very brief.

Other times there's a long return, and many things happen, which will be discussed at length in the next chapter.

The Hero Meets Evil

The hero now first prepares for, then engages in, a confrontation with the Evil One, or one of the Evil One's chief lieutenants. This confrontation almost always takes place in the lair of the Evil One—the place where the Evil One does business: office, home, palace, hideout, wherever. The Evil One's lair is sometimes called "the inmost cave."

The motif of the confrontation between the hero and the Evil One has been called the hero's "supreme ordeal," which it might well be—but not always. As an example, it might be quite an ordeal just to get to the Evil One, so it's hard to know which is supreme: the journey to get there, climbing the north face of the Eiger in dead of winter, or the confrontation itself.

Since I'm always focusing on character, I like to think of this motif of confrontation between the hero and the Evil One as more important than where it happens or the metaphor used to describe it. This is why I don't use terms like "inmost cave" or "belly of the beast," or whatever the lair of the Evil One is otherwise called.

There may be confusion over the fact that in some myth-based stories there is often a second confrontation with the Evil One on the return to the common-day world, which will be discussed later. It is the first confrontation that usually takes place in the lair of the Evil One.

- James Bond nails Dr. No in the hideout where he's firing off his rockets.

- In *From Russia with Love,* the lektor is taken from the Soviet embassy, in some sense the lair of the Evil One.

- In *Carrie,* Carrie confronts her tormentors at the prom and destroys them: this is where they were setting up their prank.

- In *The Spy Who Came in from the Cold,* there's a confrontation with the Evil One in his lair, an East German courtroom.

- Samson's first confrontation with the Evil One is when he's blinded; this happens at the Philistine king's palace, the lair of the Evil One.

- Rosie and Charley, in *The African Queen,* have a confrontation with the Evil One's representative on the *Louisa,* the Evil One's boat.

- Brody, in *Jaws,* goes to sea to have his confrontation with the evil shark in the lair of the shark, the sea.

- Ulysses confronts the cyclops in his cave, Circe in her palace, and the suitors in Ulysses's palace, which they have taken over as their own.

- In *Gone with the Wind,* the confrontation with the Evil One is symbolic: Scarlett shoots the Union soldier in her own home, which the soldier thinks is now his.

If the Hero Lives, a Prize Is Taken

During the confrontation with the Evil One, the hero often takes possession of what I call the "prize." It's sometimes called the "elixir," the "sword," the "grail," or the "McGuffin." It's the boon to be taken back to the community.

Sometimes it's not a physical thing—sometimes it's the knowledge gained or the inspiration derived from the hero's act. And sometimes—in keeping with the flexibility of myth-based fiction—there is no prize at all.

- In *From Russia with Love*, the prize is the decoding device called the "lektor."
- In *Jaws*, it's the corpse of the shark.
- In *The Old Man and the Sea*, it's the skeleton of the great fish.
- In *The African Queen*, it's the sinking of the ship *Louisa*.
- In *A Christmas Carol*, it's the spirit of Christmas, which now resides in Scrooge's heart.
- In *Lawrence of Arabia*, it's freedom for the Arabs from Turkish rule.
- In *The Spy Who Came in from the Cold*, it's getting rid of a nasty East German spy boss.

You see, there's great variety. The prize can be almost anything, as long as it's a boon to somebody.

If, in the confrontation with the Evil One, the hero is bested by the Evil One and the prize not taken, the hero will come back for the prize, and there will be a second confrontation in the lair of the Evil One. Usually the second attempt is successful if the first one failed.

If the Hero Dies

Often the confrontation with the Evil One is a duel to the death. Sometimes the Evil One dies, and sometimes the hero dies, and the story ends soon after. If either one dies, there's usually a short resolution, and that's it, end of story.

If the hero dies, usually his spirit passes on to another hero.

McMurphy, in *One Flew over the Cuckoo's Nest*, dies as a result of his confrontation with Big Nurse, but, as discussed above, the Chief is imbued with his spirit.

Another example of the spirit of the hero being passed on to another is in a pretty good mystery novel (and later film starring Omar Sharif as the hero and Peter O'Toole as the Evil One), *Night of the Generals* (1963) by Hans Hellmut Kirst, set in Nazi times. The hero is a Polish policeman. There've been a series of murders of prostitutes in the hero's jurisdiction, and the trail leads him to, you guessed it, a bigshot general. As the hero closes in on the Evil One, there's a background plot afoot to kill Hitler and have the German high command take over. Our hero invades the general's headquarters just as word has come that there's been an attempt on Hitler's life. No one knows if he's alive or dead. The hero confronts the Evil One in his office (lair of the Evil One). He tells the general he's under arrest. This general is not in on the plot to kill Hitler. At the moment the generals who are loyal to the conspirators are rounding up Hitlerites. The general pauses while they listen to a special news broadcast. Hitler is alive! The conspirators are being rounded up instead. In one of the biggest surprises in literature, the general takes a gun out and shoots our hero dead, dab-smack in the middle of the story.

But there's a lateral pass to another detective, and there's justice in the end—the boon to the community.

If the Evil One Dies

The Evil One, of course, only wins very occasionally in myth-based fiction. In the confrontation with the Evil One, the Evil One is often killed, as in Ian Fleming's *Dr. No.* In *Carrie,* one of the Evil Ones, Carrie's mother, and the hero, Carrie, both die.

If the Evil One is killed, it is usually the end of the story, but not always. Sometimes it takes great effort on the hero's part to return, even if the Evil One is no longer around. There may be mountains to climb, rivers to cross, minefields to maneuver through, and so on.

An Example: Valdez Comes

Here's how these motifs work in practice, in the flow of a story: take the film *Valdez Is Coming* (1970). This example contains the usual motifs, but they are not in the usual order. It's a great film, full of mythic resonance, based on an Elmore Leonard novel. It stars Burt Lancaster as a down-at-the-heels Mexican-American constable of the decrepit Mexican part of town. As the story opens, Valdez is in his *world of common day,* riding shotgun guard on a stage because being the constable of the Mexican part of town doesn't pay all that well. He *encounters the Evil One*, a rich gringo rancher. *The Evil One and his minions* are shooting up a small cabin with a black man and his pregnant Indian wife inside. They claim the man killed the Evil One's girlfriend's husband. The girlfriend is, of course, *Woman-as-Whore*.

Clever and resourceful, Valdez does some dangerous and tricky stuff to get close to the black man—he's hoping to bring a settlement to this dispute amicably. He is, after all, *good at what he does for a living* and willing to sacrifice himself for others. The Evil One has one of his minions sneak up behind Valdez *(the hero is betrayed)*, and the black man thinks he's been betrayed, so he opens fire on Valdez, who has to shoot him. The black man dies.

We find out then that the man was not the murderer of the Woman-as-Whore's husband, and off ride the Evil One, his girlfriend, and his minions. Valdez takes the man's pregnant Indian wife to town and tries to take up a collection for her, hoping to raise a hundred dollars to get her through the winter. Nobody wants to help her out. They say the Evil One is rich and he's responsible for her being a widow, so why not get the money from him? You guessed it, a *Threshold Guardian* warns him against such an act of tomfoolery. The hero, of course, has the *hubris* to think he can pull this off.

Valdez rides out to the Evil One's ranch, *the lair of the Evil One*, in *the Mythological Woods* for a confrontation with the Evil One. Valdez says he wants one hundred dollars *(the prize)* for the widow. The Evil One cackles and has Valdez tied to a huge cross and sent back to town on foot. It's, oh, maybe thirty miles or so, through the hot, dry desert. The hero is *wounded*, being crucified like this.

There's a creek, and Valdez is thirsty. He stumbles on the

rocks getting to the creek and lands on his back—where he can't get up or turn over. He's dying, baking to death in the sun.

Luckily, somebody comes by, that's right, to *rescue him*. He doesn't see who it is (though we find out later it was one of the Evil One's minions). This is a *death and rebirth*.

Notice, please, that the story is well told, very well structured, and the death and rebirth come after the first confrontation with the Evil One. Since the hero did not get the prize the first time, he, of course, is coming back.

Valdez gets his drink of water, reborn with a new consciousness, and stumbles into town. He goes to his rooms and opens a trunk and gets out his old army uniform for a *change of costume*. He puts on the uniform. He was once, "when he didn't know better," an army scout. He gets out his Sharp's rifle—a sniper's rifle. You guessed it, he has a *special talent* for it.

Ordinarily, the hero never goes back into the world of common day once he's left for his initiation. It works fine here because he only comes back to arm himself and to say good-bye. It doesn't work, however, when the hero tries to return to his normal life in the common-day world.

After a *tearful parting with a Loved One*—his girlfriend— he *goes back into the Mythological Woods*. On the way back to the Evil One's lair, he encounters a ranch hand, who treats him with derision and tells him to turn back. Right, *another Threshold Guardian*. Valdez scoffs, they duel, and Valdez puts a bullet in him. He tells the wounded Threshold Guardian to go to the ranch and tell them, "Valdez is coming." The hero still has his old *hubris*.

So the Evil One posts sentries, and they wait for him, underestimating the hero, of course. *The Evil One usually has a lot of hubris* as well.

Valdez, always *clever and resourceful,* sneaks into the compound, *the Evil One's lair,* with the idea of stealing the hundred dollars, *the prize.* He's caught by the *Woman-as-Whore,* who sounds the alarm. Valdez uses the Woman-as-Whore for a shield and rides off with her instead of the hundred dollars. She's the prize substitute or the real prize. The chase is on.

In the rest of the story, Valdez kills a bunch of the Evil One's minions, is tested, learns the new rules, and develops a close relationship with the Woman-as-Whore. Valdez's friend is killed (the hero often loses a Loved One).

Anyway, *Valdez Is Coming* is a good example of the monomyth in action, but in an unusual order. Works fine.

The monomyth is flexible, remember. You can use the characters and motifs in an infinite number of ways. The mythic pattern is not a straitjacket, it's Play-Doh. Have fun with it.

Back to *The Blue Light* Stepsheet

When last we left Garret, she had seen Quint being taken into Morgan Thorn's clandestine mine and was about to have a confrontation with the Evil One.

35. The preparation motif: Garret plans to go in, pretending she's lost on her own, and ask to be driven back to civilization. She carefully conceals on her person a few of her secret weapons, then rolls around in the dust so she looks as if she's been

wandering around for a couple of days. The Fool, May Jo, is there, acting the fool as usual, apparently saved from the desert once again.

36. Garret goes in and meets with Morgan Thorn, acting as if she knows nothing. She says she's looking for Quint. Morgan is most anxious to know whether anyone knows her whereabouts. He shows her his gold collection. She can see he's totally mad and realizes he's not about to let her go. But she plays along, then knocks him out when she gets her chance. With May Jo's help, she gets the keys to his vehicle and sneaks around to find Quint. She manages to free him, and they head for the car when they're overtaken by the Evil One's minions. It's now she learns that May Jo is not a Fool but rather a spy working for Morgan Thorn all along *(the hero is betrayed,* this time by *a Shape-Shifter).*

37. Garret and Quint are in a makeshift cell. With them are two university students who made the blue light for kicks with an experimental pulse laser they borrowed from the physics department. Quint is out of his head from the beating. The minions searched Garret, but failed to find all her weapons. They plan to dump all four of them in hell's living room the next day. No water for twenty miles— they'll die for sure, and no one will think it's anything but more victims of Hogan's Maze.

38. First, though, Morgan Thorn's flunkies plan to have their fun with Garret. For their trouble, they get their faces full of chemicals that blind them.

39. Garret releases the Mexican workers who are held

as virtual prisoners. They riot. Garret and the college kids start fires. Garret hot-wires a car, and off they go into Hogan's Maze. Thus, a threshold is crossed, and the third part of the hero's journey, the return, begins. This, however, is the subject of the next chapter.

8

Welcome Home, Sailor, or, The Hero Returns to the Community

The Journey Home, an Overview

The monomyth, remember, is in three sections: the separation, which takes place in the hero's world of common day; the initiation, which takes place in the Mythological Woods; and the return home, which begins on the journey home while still in the Mythological Woods, and then the threshold is crossed, and the hero is back in the world of common day. I've termed these two parts of the journey the "journey home" and the "arrival."

Often, perhaps because films are of limited duration, usually no more than a couple of hours, some parts of the monomyth are left out. The separation section in the world of common day is frequently quite short, and often there is no return at all. The hero defeats the Evil One in the confrontation, takes the prize, and that's that: the end. No journey home, no arrival.

Joseph Campbell and other mythologists have noted that there are cultural variations in the myth and that it is often telling which part of the myth is dropped. What does it say about our culture that the return to community is dropped and that the time spent with the hero in his common-day world is drastically reduced? It indicates the great importance we place on the role of the individual, and the perception that self-sacrifice for a community or an ideal is, well, sort of foolish. Sociologists have called America at this time the Me Generation. Indeed it is.

The two parts of the return, the journey home and the arrival, should not be neglected. They are important parts of the hero's journey: they are its fulfillment. The hero is seen in sharp contrast to the way he or she was before the initiation; this gives the reader a much stronger sense of what has happened to the hero and imparts meaning to the journey. Often, the return contains the most poignant and emotionally moving material when the hero either receives the reward or fails to get it. Either way, it's strong story material, and you'd be wise to exploit it.

The General Pattern of the Journey Home

The hero, following the confrontation with the Evil One, prize in hand, now heads home.

The Evil One, having lost the prize, goes after the hero.

The hero, having learned the new rules and having grown through the tests and trials, is now better equipped for the challenge of being retested on the way back.

The hero may have a second preparation scene for another confrontation with the Evil One.

The hero has another confrontation with the Evil One. In this confrontation, the hero is usually victorious. Often the Evil One is killed or captured.

The hero then crosses the threshold and arrives back in the common-day world, where yet more challenges may await. They will be discussed below.

There are variations, of course. The Evil One may kill the hero in this confrontation. The Evil One may recapture the prize, and if that happens, the hero will have to get it back. None of this is set in stone.

An Example

In *From Russia with Love*, James Bond has invaded the Soviet embassy in Istanbul (the symbolic lair of the Evil One), has stolen the lektor (the prize), and is heading home with it, taking the Hero's Lover with him. His Sidekick has been killed. The hero and his Lover get on the Orient Express and head north, the agents of Smersh after him. In this case, the real Evil One is not the Soviets after all—it's Smersh, a supersecret, private-spy agency bent on world domination.

First, Bond fights with Grant on the train and defeats him only with the help of his magic briefcase. Then, crossing the Aegean in a small boat, Bond is pursued by the Evil One's minions in small boats. He defeats them by blowing up his own reserve gas tanks—being clever and resourceful. The third and last test is while Bond, thinking he's home free, is in Venice having an idyll with his Russian lover: he's attacked by the Evil One's henchman, Olga Kreb, with a poisoned knife in her shoe. He, of course, defeats her, too, with the help of his Lover. The hero is rescued.

Like most cartoon-type monomyths, it's all in good fun. It's fun because we're never seriously worried about Bond; of course he's going to overcome the Evil One.

An exciting journey home.

- In *Gone with the Wind*, the rebuilding of Tara is Scarlett's journey home. She is severely tested, but is able to conquer because she was transformed during her initiation.
- In *The Old Man and the Sea*, a terrible thing happens on the journey home: the prize, the great fish he fought for three days, is eaten by sharks.
- Carrie's return home is short, but on the way she destroys the town.
- Huck Finn, on the way home, saves Jim the slave and foils the two con men.
- Leamas, on the journey home, overcome by feelings of betrayal at the murder of Liz, which was sanctioned by his superiors, commits suicide and never arrives.

Garret's Stepsheet Continued: The Journey Home

40. Because it's night, Garret, Quint, and the two students slowly and carefully follow the rutted tracks of the road, hoping it will show them the way out.
41. It's dawn. When Garret hot-wired the car, she cre-

ated a few shorts; now there's a small fire, and the car stops. The two college kids think they can make it to where they left their car and go for help. They leave. Garret stays behind to tend to Quint, who is fading in and out of consciousness.

42. Both Garret and Quint know that the chance they will ever get out alive is dim, that Morgan Thorn will be coming along soon with his men and he'll want to wreak a terrible vengeance. Garret prepares for the encounter by hiding Quint, piling up rocks to dump on their pursuers, draining gas out of the car's tank into some jugs she found in the trunk, and so on.

43. The second confrontation with the Evil One. Morgan has only one of his men with him, but they have shotguns and assault rifles. Garret leads them away from where she's hidden Quint, maneuvers them into a tight spot, then douses them with gasoline. They're both burned, but not killed. They manage to get back to their vehicle and leave.

44. The heat is terrible. Garret and Quint have to find shelter and water, or they will soon die. Garret is having a symbolic death. She expresses her love for Quint. Before this, she never understood the meaning of love, she says.

45. On the rock face nearby she sees the shadow of an eagle and remembers what the Woman-as-Goddess told her in her dream. She goes to a crack in the rock where the eagle is pointing and finds the lost Hogan's well, and they have all the cool, fresh water they could want.

46. Refreshed, Garret sends up smoke signals, and
    soon they hear a helicopter coming. Thayer is in
    the helicopter. Garret and Quint are whisked off
    to a hospital.

Next, the arrival home, the last part of the hero's journey.

The Arrival Home

The hero starts for home, crossing over another threshold,
and lands dab-smack in the middle of the world of common
day. Here, various things might happen.

Some heroes are awarded a hero's welcome. Scrooge gets
the hero's welcome as soon as he starts making merry.

In *The Old Man and the Sea*, there's a great example of
the return dramatically exploited. Santiago, the old man, has
gone in a small skiff out into the Mythological Woods, the
swiftest part of the Gulf Stream, where he has never gone
before. Here he must learn the new rules, and he is tested
mightily in catching the great fish. Many critics have claimed
that Santiago's sufferings are much like Christ's. The fish
line cuts into his back as if he were scourged, his hands are
cut by the line and are bloodied, and so on. The old man's
fight with the great fish, they say, is emblematic of Christ's
fight against Satan (the Evil One). Hemingway denied this
vociferously. And he never heard of the monomyth, yet he
created a monomythic gem. Santiago, after his great struggle, takes the prize and heads home. But along the way he
is attacked by sharks, and the prize is taken from him. All
he has left when he returns is the skeleton. But he is re-

warded a hero's triumphal return, for everyone can see what a mighty fish it must have been. Santiago has earned back his manhood.

Other heroes aren't so lucky. The prize might be seen as a great thing, or the prize may not be appreciated. Yup, the whole thing may have been for naught, as far as the community is concerned. The Chief's busting out of the cuckoo's nest wouldn't be appreciated by most communities, who think it's a boon to keep the nuts in the cuckoo's nest.

The prize may be snatched away from the hero at the last moment.

Leamas never gets back for his hero's welcome: he and Liz die going over the wall.

Carrie's mother is waiting to shove a knife into her when she gets home.

A false hero may claim the hero's reward. Doesn't happen often, but it does happen.

The hero's return may bring more conflict, strife, and terrible trouble.

When Michael Corleone returns home, the boon he brings is his own transformation. He's now ready to lead his community, his "family," on a war of revenge against the other five Mafia families in New York. It is to Puzo's great credit that he skillfully has brought the reader along with the hero, cheering every moment as this war hero is turned into a crime lord.

Garret Arrives Back Home:
The Stepsheet Continues

47. Back in the world of the common day, Garret sees to it that Quint is okay before going to work. As he comes around, he asks her not to destroy everyone's dreams by revealing that the blue light was only a hoax. She says she can't do that—she's sorry, but she's a reporter and she reports the news.

48. At Garret's apartment house, the old lady desert rat congratulates her—a celebration.

49. At work, Garret finds that her young colleague, Fred Hanson, whom she'd conned out of taking the assignment, has already written up the big story of the hidden mine—after all, deadlines must be met. In the story, she's lauded as a hero. He got the story from the two college kids, who didn't tell him they perpetrated the hoax; after all, they "borrowed" the equipment and wouldn't like to face the consequences. Morgan Thorn, meanwhile, is in a hospital ward at the city jail, charged with 158 felonies, and every reporter in the state is writing about him and his slave operation in the desert. Morgan seems to revel in the publicity.

50. She sits down to write the exposé of the blue light, but can't bring herself to do it. She just can't destroy everyone's dreams (the journey has transformed her). Instead, she writes the story of how the blue light affected different people, how

it brought hope and how it brought people together. How it led people to love. Marion, her
editor, says it's her best work since her "Only a
Maid" story.

51. Garret visits Quint in the hospital. He's with
Thayer, who's been transformed by her journey as
well and is no longer Woman-as-Bitch. Quint is
much improved—he's read Garret's story and is
impressed. He talks about how he's going to teach
her to ride a horse, and how much she's going to
love Paradise Valley in the high country, his favorite spot on the face of the earth. She gets caught
up in his dreams.

52. The next morning, the big news comes: Garret has
been offered a job on the *New York Times*. Wow,
she's ecstatic; she quits her job at the *Westerner* and
starts packing.

53. Quint shows up on crutches; he's heard the news.
Garret asks him to come to New York, even
though she knows it could never work. He's not a
New York kind of guy. She promises they'll see
each other often—she will be getting a month's
vacation every year, and they can go to Paradise
Valley. He says he's spoken to Marion Weibel,
who will give her her old job back. Quint says he
doesn't mind having a wife who works; he believes
people should do what makes them happy. She's
sorry, she says, Reno just isn't her idea of living,
and she's not the marrying kind.

54. Garret kisses Quint good-bye and starts crying.
She never cries, she says. He doesn't either, he says.

But he looks as if he's about to start. She promises
to phone him as soon as she gets to New York and
rushes out the door.

The end.

A Checklist for the Hero's Journey

The following checklist might help you to keep the heroic
qualities and motifs in mind as you work on your stepsheet
for your myth-based story.

At the beginning, the hero always:

is a protagonist (or becomes a protagonist in the course
of the story), which means he or she will take the
lead in a cause or action;

has courage (or finds it in the course of the story);

is an "outlaw" (a maverick of some kind) living by his
or her own code;

is good at what he or she does for a living;

has one or more special talents;

is motivated by idealism (at least at some point in the
story);

has been "wounded" (maimed, disgraced, grieving for
a lost loved one, etc.);

is clever and resourceful;

is sexually potent;

takes action—is not just a passive observer for very
long.

In the course of the story, the hero never:

quits,
acts cruelly,
whines,
grovels, or
wins by luck (though luck may play a part).

The hero usually:

is stoical;
is loyal;
is forgiving (or learns to forgive in the course of the
     story);
is considered sexually appealing;
is physically superior in some way (strength, speed,
     hearing, reflexes, etc.);
has a special birth (a parent might be a king, a doomed
     prisoner, a goddess, an Apache warrior, and the
     like);
has a special destiny (predicted by a seer, perhaps).

The hero sometimes:

is cynical;
is mouthy—known as a wise guy if a man; sharp-
     tongued, if a woman;
has a cohero who is also on a heroic journey (as in the
     case of *The African Queen*);
has one or more Sidekicks who are heroic but less tal-

ented than the hero (Tonto, Robin, Little John, the
Tin Man, Dr. Watson);

has a Magical Helper (Tinker Bell, Q, Paul Drake, Jim-
iny Cricket, healers, the PI's friend in the police
department);

has followers (the men of Sherwood, Jason's Argonauts,
Ulysses's crew), but is always outnumbered and out-
gunned by the opposition, i.e. the Evil One.

In the world of the everyday, the hero:

will be engaged in conflict;

will receive a "call to adventure";

will "disintegrate" (be ostracized, become depressed
and/or bitter, may turn to drink, and so on) if he
or she refuses the call to adventure;

may consult with a Wise One who will give sage advice;

may go to a Magical Helper who will give him or her
"magic" for the journey (spells, amulets, science, secret weapon, etc.);

may have a tearful parting with a Loved One;

may be forced to go on the journey against his or her
will;

may receive (and will ignore) a warning not to go on
the journey from a Threshold Guardian.

On the journey, the hero will undergo an "initiation" in
the Mythological Woods during which the hero:

will have to learn the new rules;

will be tested, overcoming internal limitations;

will show a willingness to give his/her life for others or for a cause;

will have a death-and-rebirth experience (at least symbolically);

will be opposed by the Evil One, who will probably have powerful allies (note: the Evil One may have many heroic qualities such as great strength, stoicism, courage, and so on, but is usually cruel and motivated not by idealism, but by his or her own ego);

may be rescued once by other characters or by divine intervention, but rarely more than once;

may attend a celebration, usually with drinking and dancing; sometimes as the guest of honor;

may change his or her "uniform" or otherwise alter his or her appearance;

may often face universal fears: heights, fire, wild animals, creepy things, dark places, claustrophobic spaces, water (storms at sea, rapids, the depths of the sea, and so on), high speeds, physical combat, inhospitable environments, monsters, spirits, and so on;

may enter an altered state of consciousness one or more times (be drugged, get drunk, go into a trance, be bewitched, and so on);

may use magic (in modern stories, high-tech devices);

may have magic used against him/her;

may fall in love;

may rescue someone held captive;

may be betrayed;

may be "marked" (branded, tattooed, maimed, or scarred);

may be a Shape-Shifter;

may encounter Shape-Shifters (Circe the witch, the Glenn Close character in *Fatal Attraction*, the wicked stepmother in *Snow White*);

may encounter a Trickster;

may lose an ally to death;

may encounter a Fool, whom no one but the hero recognizes as wise;

may encounter women in one or more of the following guises: "Mother," "Goddess," "Nymph (pixie)," "Crone," "Whore," "Bitch," "Femme Fatale" (note: the Hero's Sidekick, the Wise One, the Evil One, the Trickster, and so on, may also be women);

may encounter a God with Clay Feet.

At the end of the initiation, the hero:

will prepare for a confrontation with the Evil One;

will have a confrontation with the Evil One, or a powerful ally of the Evil One, in the Evil One's lair (castle, fort, mansion, office, and so on);

may take possession of a "prize" in the Evil One's lair, which will benefit his community—a medicine, magic, the Holy Grail, a spy's decoder ring, advanced knowledge, etc.;

will either die or be triumphant in the confrontation with the Evil One;

will, if triumphant, begin the return to his or her own community.

On the return, the hero:

may be opposed by minions of the Evil One, the Evil One himself, or others, who wish to prevent the hero from returning;

may experience or reexperience some of the initiation process, such as being scarred, being betrayed, changing consciousness, falling in love, losing an ally to death, and so on;

may encounter the same mythological cast as during the initiation: the Fool, the Trickster, Woman as Crone, Whore, Bitch, and so on;

may lose the prize and have to retrieve it;

may have another death-and-rebirth experience;

may have another confrontation with the Evil One, or a powerful ally of the Evil One, sometimes without preparation, usually not in the Evil One's lair;

may not be able to retrieve the prize (e.g., the sharks taking the great fish from the old man in *The Old Man and the Sea*).

Back in the world of common day, the hero:

will demonstrate that he or she has been transformed by the experience of the journey (this will always be indicated, no matter how short the return);

may find the prize is not seen for the boon that it is;

may have to contend with a false hero who claims the
    hero's reward and honor;

may not be appreciated for the sacrifices he or she has
    made and the suffering he or she has endured;

may be reunited with a Loved One;

may learn from the Wise One the meaning of the jour-
    ney;

may get a call to begin a new adventure.

There it is, the entire hero's journey. There are two special cases of the hero's journey—the tragic hero and the comic hero—which come next. Also, some sage advice and a great example of the hero's journey that the fiction writer takes.

9

Of Tragic Heroes and Comic Heroes and Other Stuff

The Tragic Death of the Standard Hero

There are two types of tragic hero. The first type is simply a standard hero who dies.

Usually the hero dies at the hands of the Evil One, often in the confrontation with the Evil One in the Evil One's lair at the end of the initiation. But it may happen later, on the return, or even after arriving back at home.

When the standard hero dies, it often comes as a shock to the reader. After all, the hero is supposed to be victorious. When Joseph Campbell in *The Hero with a Thousand Faces* described the monomyth, he said (as quoted in the introduction): "A hero ventures forth from the world of common day into a region of supernatural wonder: fabulous forces are there encountered and a decisive victory is won: the hero comes back from this mysterious adventure with the power to bestow boons on his fellow man."

Note that he says, "a decisive victory is won." This does not mean that the hero necessarily survives.

- McMurphy, in *One Flew over the Cuckoo's Nest*, dies. In his conflict with the Evil One, Big Nurse, he is lobotomized and then smothered to death by his allies because being lobotomized is a fate worse than death. Even so, he is victorious because his spirit lives on in Chief, who then smashes his way out of the cuckoo's nest.
- In the very fine film *Hombre* (1967), based on an Elmore Leonard novel, the hero has a shoot-out with the Evil One on the return and is killed, but so is the Evil One and his Sidekick, so the hero is victorious. And the loot will be returned to the starving Indians from whom it was stolen.
- Carrie, too, is victorious before she dies. She wreaks her revenge on the boys who dump pig blood on her. She kills them and, for good measure, wipes out the rest of the class and much of the town with her psychic powers.
- In Hemingway's magnificent novel *For Whom the Bell Tolls*, Jordan, the hero, is killed while blowing up the bridge. The hero dies, but the mission is accomplished—a victory is won.

This is the point of the death of the standard hero: if the standard hero is to die, he will die victorious.

Sometimes the standard hero dies, not at the hands of the Evil One or his minions, but at the hands of his friends, followers, or kinsmen. Such was the case in a fine film about the war for Israeli independence, *Cast a Giant Shadow* (1966), where the hero, after helping his army take the prize (the liberation of Jerusalem), is shot by a sentry because he does not know the Hebrew password.

The Doomed Hero

There's another kind of tragic hero. He is not simply a standard hero who doesn't make it back. Let's call him the "doomed hero." A sense of gloom clings to this tragic hero right from the beginning. This hero is usually not victorious.

The doomed hero is severely wounded—so wounded that he or she often is being driven mad. Hamlet is of this type. So are Macbeth and Othello. Tess, in Thomas Hardy's *Tess of the D'Urbervilles* (1891), is a female version; so is Saint Joan in Shaw's play.

Such doomed heroes brood a great deal, and they are often bitter and full of remorse. No one understands them. They are frequently thought to be insane.

Sometimes the doomed hero's wound is self-inflicted. The hero may have committed some great sin or great crime and may not be able to muster the courage to do whatever his or her conscience tells the hero he or she must do to fix it.

Sometimes the doomed hero commits the sin before our very eyes, and no matter how hard he or she tries, the sin cannot be expiated. Anna Karenina and Madame Bovary are two examples. They have both committed adultery.

Often the doomed hero's sin is that of cowardice: the hero has had a failure of nerve. Hamlet, as an example, hasn't the courage to kill his uncle, the king, who killed Hamlet's father and married Hamlet's mother.

Or the sin might be that the doomed hero committed

some terrible act of betrayal. Macbeth betrays his king and, later, his friends and allies. He has his best friend, Banquo, killed.

The tragic hero of this sort is often in league with the Evil One, rather than in opposition to the Evil One. In *Macbeth*, the Evil One is Lady Macbeth. Macbeth believes every dark word she utters. Othello believes Iago, who is plotting his ruin.

In these types of tragedy, the death of the doomed hero is quite different from that of the standard hero, who dies victorious. The reader or audience of such a tragedy does not say at the end, "Gee, isn't it awful that the hero died after achieving his victory?" nor does he or she feel both the sense of victory and the sadness of death.

In the case of the doomed hero, the feeling is more like "Isn't it tragic that this person, who could have been a hero, became instead a villain?" Such a hero is not worthy of our sympathy or even pity: the pity we have for such heroes is contempt.

Frequently, such heroes die or are maimed by their own hand because they have an inherent personality defect. Sonny, in *The Godfather*, is such a tragic figure. He's killed because he's hotheaded and easily trapped. Othello was paranoid. Emma Bovary was blinded by her lust for the good life.

Aristotle, in *The Poetics* (fourth century B.C.), wrote that the only possible tragedy was in seeing the downfall of the high and mighty, that the audience experienced "awe" and "pity," and had a sort of purging of their pent-up emotion as a result. It was "cathartic," which was the very point. The audience watching a tragedy was purged; the soul was re-freshed.

The brooding, self-destructive hero may sometimes be re-deemed in the end by seeking forgiveness or by performing a truly self-sacrificing act. Sometimes such doomed heroes per-form the self-sacrificing act too late and are killed by a former ally or kinsman. Often, too, such tragic figures may welcome death: their wound hurts so much that they'd rather die.

The Comic Hero

The comic hero is often a good-hearted person who wants to do good, who in fact would like to be a hero, and who sometimes even thinks of himself or herself as heroic, but, alas, does not measure up. The comic hero is frequently a buffoon.

The comic hero may be wounded, but it's usually his or her fault.

As I pointed out above, a character in a myth-based story may take on more than one mythic role. The Lover, as an example, may also be the Sidekick. Or the Loved One of the Tearful Good-bye may also be the Threshold Guardian. In the case of the comic hero, we have a fusion of the hero and the Fool. Jerry Lewis made a career out of playing such a character. So did Lou Costello, who with his partner, Bud Abbot, was for a time making the highest-grossing films in Hollywood and who lives on today on TV. The title char-acter of Cervantes's *Don Quixote* (1615), often credited with being the first novel, was such a character. So was Jacques

Clouseau, the comic hero of the Pink Panther film series
starring Peter Sellers. The film *Forest Gump* (1997), winner
of the Academy Award for Best Picture, was about a Fool
as hero.

The comic hero may or may not be courageous. The Lou
Costello character was often a coward; so were the characters
played by Jerry Lewis. But other examples of the comic hero,
like Clouseau, are courageous. Rather, they're too dumb to
know fear.

In many other ways, the comic hero is simply the standard
hero turned upside down:

- The real hero is good at what he does for a living.
  The comic hero is a bungler. Clouseau, as a detective,
  is an idiot and such a bungler that he drives his boss,
  Commissioner Dreyfus, to insanity.
- The real hero has a special talent. The comic hero
  normally has no talent and may even have a special
  liablity. Clouseau, as an example, is as clumsy as a
  newborn colt. There are exceptions, however: Forest
  Gump could run like the wind.
- The comic hero may whine and grovel; the true hero
  may not.
- The comic hero may win by luck; the true hero never
  does.
- The comic hero is rarely stoical, but, like a true hero,
  is loyal and forgiving. The comic hero, remember, has
  a good heart.
- Unlike the true hero, the comic hero is rarely sexually
  appealing, though he or she may think so.
- The comic hero is rarely physically superior (Forest

Gump being a notable exception). In fact, comic heroes are often physically inferior.

- The comic hero may be mistaken for a true hero and therefore may be marked or have a special birth, or think so.
- Upon the return, the comic hero often claims the reward of the true hero, who usually lets the comic hero have the credit. In *The Pink Panther*, this motif was stretched to the limit when the phantom, the jewel thief, turns the tables on Clouseau, who is convicted of the crime. Clouseau, reveling in the notoriety, takes the credit.
- On the journey, the comic hero will encounter the same cast of characters as a real hero, and the journey will feature the same motif—except that there is no transformation in the comic hero. The very point of the comic hero's adventure is that he or she does not have the transformation that a hero should experience. At the end of the journey, Clouseau is still the same old Clouseau.

A Final Note About *The Blue Light*

You may have noticed that the premise I set out to prove with *The Blue Light* was not proved. Love did not conquer ambition. The end of the story I indicated in the previous chapter, of course, is not the end of the story. Here is the actual ending, picking up with Garret as she leaves for the airport. This time I won't give you the steps; I'll just show you the final scenes.

THE BLUE LIGHT

Chapter 45 (or thereabouts)

Garret made a deal with Fred Hanson for her car. She let him have it for well under the market price, and, in gratitude, he agreed to drive her to the airport.

"Imagine, the New York Times," he said, as he loaded her single, carry-on bag into the trunk. She carried her laptop in a leather shoulder bag. "The New York Times," he said again, with awe in his voice, his eyes rolling toward heaven.

A gust of hot, dusty wind swirled around them, and an image of Quint holding her as the dust storm raged around her passed by her mind.

"We better hurry; we'll miss the plane." She tossed him the keys. "You drive."

She'd have somebody else pack the rest of her things later and ship them, as soon as she found an apartment in Greenwich Village or Soho. She'd get a one bedroom, she figured. She'd have to buy a lot of new clothes. *You have to look sharp when you work for the* Times, she thought. She was hoping to get the police beat; there was always a lot of action there. The real drama, that was right up her alley. But city hall would be good too. Anything, just as long as she could breathe the air of Manhattan.

She shut her eyes and pictured it, glittering in the night. Pulsing with life.

They drove two blocks to the freeway entrance. The afternoon traffic was light. Garret looked over at the cluster of casinos downtown and the big one out by the airport standing alone. Casinos and restaurants and bars and bowling alleys, surrounded by a whole lot of sand and rock. What a town. Crammed with tourists, all dumping coins in little boxes that beep and bonk and flash lights and have little windows with JACKPOT written on them. God, she couldn't wait to get out of this town.

And then she saw the sign for the Lucky Deuces. Wasn't that where Quint said he played? She turned her eyes away. Her heart suddenly felt as if it was beating out of time, and her face felt flush.

"You okay?" Fred Hanson asked.

"Fine."

"Is that a tear on your cheek?"

She touched her cheek and felt moisture. "Have something in my eye."

"It's the dust."

After a moment, he said, "That fellow Quint you were stuck in the desert with, what was he like?"

"I don't know. Nice. Your typical cowboy, big, strong, and friendly."

"I saw the TV interview with you and him. He sure couldn't keep his eyes off you."

"Would you please just drive."

"Okay. Sorry, I didn't know."

"Didn't know what?"

"That you kind of fell for him."

"Christ, would you just drive and mind your own business."

"Sorry, again."

In a few minutes they were getting off the freeway and circling into the airport and pulling up in front of the terminal. He said, "Being a reporter for the *Times* means a lot to you, doesn't it, Garret?"

"It means everything."

He nodded. "I see. . . ."

"Mind your own damn business."

She got out of the car. He opened the trunk and took out her bag. "I made a mistake once just like the one you're making now. When I went to grad school at Cal . . . there was this girl, Jenny, her name was."

"You don't understand, Fred. I'm not the type to marry and raise brats—that's his idea of the good life. He rides horses, goes off into the desert for weeks at a time. He doesn't even have a damn job, let alone a profession or a career . . . never mind." She grabbed her bag. "Look, you be good to Marion and everybody at the *Westerner*; they're wonderful people. You've got it in you to be a good reporter, Fred. I think you'll make it."

He shook her hand. "Thanks, Garret, you've got it in you to be a great one."

She gave him a hug, they said their good-byes, and she hurried into the terminal. She went to the counter and checked in and got her seat assignment. She had to hurry; the plane was due to leave in five minutes.

Garret ran down the corridor past slot machines and signs advertising casinos and clubs, looking around, hoping . . . hoping for what? That Quint might have been psychic enough to know which flight she'd booked? That he'd come to see her off and play the tearful good-bye scene again? *Couldn't stand that,* she thought.

She got on the plane and took her seat halfway back on the window side. The plane was nearly full of passengers—she was lucky, she thought, to have an empty seat next to her.

She could see out the window that they were still loading the luggage. She leaned back and shut her eyes and told herself to relax. She'd call Quint when she got to New York. It wasn't over; she'd see him again. They'd have one of those bicoastal relationships. They'd meet in the middle of the country maybe. And often.

That would have to do. She just wasn't the ranch-wife type, and that was all there was to it. She was a *New York Times* reporter. *New York Times* hotshot newshound. All she needed was a chance to dig her teeth into a big story. Some day, there'd be a Pulitzer.

She turned and looked toward the mountains shimmering in the distance. She could make out the twin peaks Quint said marked the entrance to Paradise Valley, where he, no doubt, would have wanted to go for their honeymoon. Sleep on the ground with coyotes howling. . . .

Cuddling in a sleeping bag beneath the stars.

Strange, but there was something in the sky above the peaks . . . a shaft of light, blue light.

But that wasn't possible. The blue light apparatus had been smashed. She rubbed her eyes—this was ridiculous.

Garret stood up and asked a couple of nuns in the row behind her if they could see the two peaks. They looked and said they could.

"What do you see above them?"

"Clouds," one said.

"And sky," said the other.

She sat back down and looked again. If anything, the shaft of deep blue light was larger than before, even in daylight.

Daylight. It had never appeared in daylight before. Never. How could it? It just wasn't possible.

She checked with a couple more passengers, but nobody else could see it.

Garret stood up in the aisle and laughed out loud.

A flight attendant came up to her. "Is something wrong, ma'am?"

"Yes, I've gone stark, raving mad. Isn't it wonderful? Stop the presses, I'm getting off!"

She made it to the front of the plane just as they were closing the door and dashed across the ramp, then followed the signs to the rental car companies.

Garret found the country road, but twice missed the turn to Twin Pines. It turned out to be a gravel road. The sun was low in the mountains as she drove the rented Ford Taurus through the old wooden entrance of Buster's Rancho, the name burned into a log on the side of the road. The driveway was rutted and bumpy, and there was a wooden fence with high, sand-colored sagebrush on either side. She rolled down the window and smelled the warm, fresh air.

Her heart was beating fast, and her thoughts were all jumbled up. This was going to be her home until death do them part. It was like the moon. It was crazy. It was dumb, to throw away the chance of a lifetime to get a crack at the big time in New York. She had an impulse to turn around, to get back on the plane. . . .

Then Garret crested a small rise, and there it was before her: the barn, a corral with a few horses, and a small, cozy house with a big, shady porch with a swing on it.

There was someone on the swing reading a book . . . Quint!

And suddenly it felt so right.

She drove up to the house and stopped the car and got out. Quint stood up and went to the railing, a look of astonishment on his face. She came over to him, feeling somewhat dizzy.

"My God," he said, "is everything all right?"

"I, ah, was on the plane," she said, her voice choking, "but then I saw this strange apparition in the sky."

"You're trembling all over."

"I saw a shaft of blue light over Paradise Valley. Nobody else could see it. It's really true, just like you've said all along, the blue light is in each of us."

He came around the railing and put his arms around her. "But what about the *Times*? Manhattan?"

"No blue light there."

"But what'll you do here?"

"First thing," she said, "I guess I've got to learn to ride a horse."

And she kissed him and felt the warm glow of a blue light all around them.

The End

This is the real end. This is a draft, of course. When I started the scenario for *The Blue Light*, I had no intention of writing it as a novel. But the more I worked on it, the more I liked it. It just might become a novel someday.

The Mythic Journey of the Writer

As we all know, one of the purposes of literature is instruction. It is certainly true of the myth-based stories. Witnessing fictional heroes being courageous in battle has inspired many a man and many a boy to go off to war. John Wayne is the father of a million heroes.

In chapter 2 of this book, the purpose of the monomyth in common-day life was discussed through the Jungian theory; how the pattern of transformation of the hero, planted deep in the brain mass of all of us and reinforced by hearing and reading myth-based stories, will come to our aid when we need to change.

Myth is the matrix out of which culture is built. Myths and legends combine to form a sort of mythological soup that is the mythos of a people. This mythos is the software of culture. When you write myth-based, heroic fiction, you are contributing to the mythos of Western civilization and, perhaps, of the entire world.

Heroic fiction is the model on which the pattern of human striving and transformation is built. As discussed in chapter 1, Carl Jung, the psychologist, saw the unconscious mind as having both an individual unconscious and a "collective unconscious," common to all human beings on the planet. He claimed there was an inherited architecture of the mind that predisposed people to be receptive to the elements of myths. The functions of myth, in his view, correspond to the archetypes in the collective unconscious.

Myth is important to culture because it is through our

identification with heroes—as super role models—that we aspire to achieve things beyond their self-serving, ego-gratifying natures. It is because of the heroes who are our models that we see ourselves as heroic when the time comes to be heroic.

Joseph Campbell used to ask why a man would jump off a bridge into the rapids to save a stranger. Or run into a burning house. On the news and in newspapers there are often accounts of heroes risking their lives for strangers. When they are asked afterward why they did it, the heroes often say they don't know. They frequently say they are not heroes, that they just did what anyone else would have done in the same circumstances.

Campbell's answer to this phenomenon was that, in the moment of crisis, the dividing line between the person in distress and the hero about to jump into the rapids or rush into the flames vanishes, and the hero sees that we are all one—in the sense that the Eastern mystics use the term. Jung, I guess, would say that at that moment the hero is overwhelmed by the collective unconscious.

I don't think that's what happens at all. I think that with the image of the mythical hero in mind, the real-life rescuer assumes the role of the hero; the rescuer takes on the mantle of the hero that has been reinforced by a thousand stories that he or she has lived through vicariously.

Identification, the mysterious ability people have to live inside the thoughts, feelings, and actions of others, is what allows people to dream the fictive dream. This identification with the hero creates a shared consciousness with the hero on his or her journey. The hero and the reader are one. In time of stress, this hero consciousness that resides in people breaks through from the unconscious to the conscious. I believe that when the real-life hero runs into the burning building, he or she is under the spell of personal heroes. He or she is James Bond, Indiana Jones, Superwoman, Wonder Woman, Xena, Tarzan, Joan of Arc, John Wayne. The hero, if Jung is correct, is not just out there, remember, but is an archetype, an inborn part of the structure of the mind; and because of this, we are not passive participants in the lives of heroes—the heroes are in us.

Heroes, it has been said, are outlaws, nonconformists, rebels, because they are taking our culture to new places, into unknown territories where the conformists, in their buttoned-down world, don't want to go. You, as a writer, must see to it that your heroes do go where, as they say on *Star Trek,* "no one has gone before." This is the challenge of the creative life.

As a creator of myth-based fiction, you have an obligation to your reader. Myth-based fiction is moral by its very nature. The hero is never cruel, never evil; the hero acts out of unselfish motives. The characters we create and their actions are a part of the mythos and, as such, potentially have an enormous impact on people, culture, and, perhaps, even history.

You, as the mythopoet, have your hand on the tiller of history and are steering its course. You have the potential to change the world.

I'm ending this book with a story about the fiction writer on the hero's journey.

The Monster of the Imagination

When a fiction writer first starts to write fiction, he or she often becomes quickly enchanted by the music of his or her freshly created prose and at the same time is frequently deeply troubled by the powerful emotions that writing fiction arouses. Just as actors must stir emotions in themselves to breathe life into their performances, so fiction writers must stir their own emotions in order to breathe life into their characters. These emotions pull the fiction writer in the direction of unexplored territory, into the dark woods of the imagination, a place of terror.

Timid at first, the fiction writer does not venture far into the woods. Here, at the outer edges of the woods where it feels safe, the fiction writer's work is often overly cerebral, dull. Fearing to go deeply into the dark woods, he or she soon develops an aesthetic blindness and cannot see the bloodlessness of these creations. Instead, the fiction writer celebrates them, seeing in these emaciated works his surface reflection mirrored there.

The blindness, though, is temporary. Rejection, criticism in creative writing workshops, the pained expressions on the faces of friends who read these deeply flawed works, force the writer to press on into unknown territory where the woods are thick and nearly impenetrable. The writer is distressed to find that there are no signposts, no paths, no tracks to follow, because this is the woods of his or her own imagination, where no one else has ever been before.

Now deeply inside the woods, the fiction writer hears

mysterious sounds of heavy breathing, the rustling of branches, howls and shrieks that freeze the fiction writer in his or her tracks. Suddenly, from out of the darkness appears a fire-breathing monster as big as a mountain. Trembling with fear, the fiction writer reaches for a quiver of arrows: reason, logic, hard work, persistence, a knowledge of language, a storehouse of reading, lessons learned from living. Arrows that have slain many monsters in the ordinary world with a single shot through the heart.

The fiction writer's aim is true, and the sharp-tipped arrows sink deep into the monster's thick hide, but the monster only roars with laughter, for this is the monster of the fiction writer's own imagination, which is unlike any monster he or she has faced in the ordinary world. This monster is fueled with the fiction writer's own emotions, fears, guilts, memories, and pain, and hence cannot be defeated with ordinary weapons.

The fiction writer turns and flees from the woods in panic.

Once back in the ordinary world, he or she reads about other writers who have gone before, hoping to find some weapon that will slay the monster. By studying the masters, the fiction writer builds confidence. From the masters, the fiction writer learns some of the monster's strange habits of feeding on the flesh of fiction writers and discovers that this can be endured.

By seeking lessons and inspiration from the masters, the fiction writer tries to imitate them, not only in their forms, but in their styles and voices as well. He or she, perhaps, finds a popular writer and creates an imitation of the writer's work, changing but a few outward trappings to avoid the accusation of plagiarism.

Writing imitations may bring some success, but even this success will not soothe the vague guilts arising in the dead of night. No matter how skillful the fiction writer becomes at copying the masters, there is no satisfaction to be found in this endeavor.

It is now, in desperation, that the fiction writer seeks wisdom from guides who have gone deep into the dark woods themselves. It is from these guides that the fiction writer learns this truth: the monster cannot be killed.

If the monster cannot be killed, how, then, can progress be made? the fiction writer demands to know.

The guides say nothing whatever on this point. Their advice is always of a technical nature—write truthfully, try to make it real, make it universal yet unique, try to plumb the depths of your characters and make them face the dilemmas of their own existence. The real message remains unsaid. Hints are metaphorical, messages about truth and self and real knowledge, messages that the fiction writer can't quite grasp. It is through trial and error that the fiction writer finally apprehends the nature of the dilemma—the monster may not be slain, but it can be ridden. The saddle is small and covered with burrs, and the monster will not take a bit; but still, if the fiction writer dares to climb aboard, it is possible.

The fiction writer is ready then to enter the woods once more, determined to find the monster and climb aboard the monster's back. Heading straight into the darkest part of the woods, the writer senses that the monster is there, waiting, breathing fire hot enough to melt steel.

It is a wild ride, as the monster crashes through the trees, trampling everything in its path. Here, other monsters are encountered and stand in the way; the fiction writer must confront each one and overcome it through hand-to-hand combat. These are the monsters hidden deep in the well of the fiction writer's own creative imagination. These monsters are the fiction writer's own secret selves, unrecognized. The battles are hard and bloody, and the fiction writer is often exhausted, but victories are won.

Talent and hard work will smooth the path, but the only way to succeed is to keep riding the monster on whichever path he takes—for they all lead to the truth of the fiction writer's own selfhood—a place where the hot springs of creativity bubble up through the forest floor. It is here, at the center of his or her own selfhood, that the fiction writer finds all that can be known about being a human being. It is here, scarred and bleeding from the battles fought along the path, that the fiction writer finds the truth that is the source, not of fiction that is simply pleasing and publishable, but fiction that aspires to the level of high art.

Bibliography

Aristotle. *The Poetics.* in *The Complete Works of Aristotle: The Revised Oxford Translation*, Jonathan Barnes, ed. Princeton, N.J.: Princeton University Press, 1983.

Austen, Jane. *Pride and Prejudice.* New York: Modern Library, 1996.

———. *Northanger Abbey.* New York: Penguin USA, 1996.

Baum, Frank L. *The Wizard of Oz.* New York: Henry Holt & Company, Inc., 1988.

Benchley, Peter. *Jaws.* New York: Doubleday and Company, Inc., 1974.

Campbell, Joseph. *Hero With a Thousand Faces.* Princeton, N.J.: Princeton University Press, 1948.

Cervantes (Miguel De Cervantes Saavedra). *Don Quixote.* Translated by Samuel Putnam. New York: The Modern Library, 1988.

Clancy, Tom. *Clear and Present Danger.* New York: Putnam Pub Group, 1989.

———. *Patriot Games.* Berkley Pub Group, 1992.

————. *Hunt for Red October.* New York: Berkley Pub Group, 1997.

Cleage, Pearl. *What Looks Like Crazy on an Ordinary Day.* New York: Avon Books, 1999.

Collins, Tess. *The Law of Revenge.* New York, Ivy Books, 1997.

————. *The Law of the Dead.* New York: Ivy Books, 1999.

Conrad, Joseph. *Lord Jim.* Garden City, N.Y.: Doubleday, Doran & Company, Inc., 1941.

Corman, Avery. *Kramer vs. Kramer.* New York: New Reader's Press, 1989.

Crane, Stephen. *The Red Badge of Courage.* New York: The New American Library, 1960.

Day, Martin S. *The Many Meanings of Myth.* Lanham, M.D.: University Press of America, Inc., 1984.

Dickens, Charles. *A Christmas Carol.* New York: Simon and Schuster, 1939.

Dostoevsky, Fyodor. *Crime and Punishment.* Translated by Constance Garnett. New York: A & C Boni., 1933.

————. *The Idiot.* Translated with an introduction by David Magarshacks. Harmandsworth, England: Penguin Books, 1975.

Egri, Lajos. *The Art of Dramatic Writing.* New York: Simon and Schuster, 1946.

Flaubert, Gustave. *Madame Bovary.* Translated by Lowell Bair. New York: Bantam Books, 1959.

Fleming, Ian. *Goldfinger.* New York: Macmillan & Co., 1959.

————. *From Russia With Love.* New York: Macmillan & Co., 1957.

Ford, Richard. *The Sportswriter.* New York: Random House, 1986.

Forrester, C. S. *The African Queen.* New York: Little Brown & Co. (1984).

Frazier, Charles. *Cold Mountain.* New York: Atlantic Monthly Press, 1997.

Frey, James *How to Write a Damn Good Novel*. New York: St. Martin's Press, 1987.

———. *How to Write a Damn Good Novel, II: Advanced Techniques for Dramatic Storytelling*. New York: St. Martin's Press, 1994.

Goethe, Johann Wolfgang von. *The Sorrows of Young Werther*. New York: Viking Press, 1989.

Grisham, John. *The Firm*. New York: Island Books, 1992.

Hardy, Thomas. *Tess of the D'Urbervilles*. New York: The Modern Library, 1932.

Hemingway, Ernest. *For Whom the Bell Tolls*. New York: Charles Scribner's Sons, 1940.

———. *The Old Man and the Sea*. New York: Charles Scribner's Sons, 1952.

———. *The Sun Also Rises*. New York: Modern Library, 1926.

Hinton, S. E. *Taming the Star Runner*. New York: Delacorte Press, 1988.

Hooker, Richard. *M*A*S*H*. New York: Pocket Books, Inc., 1969.

Hugo, Victor. *Les Misérables*. Translated by Norman Denny. New York: Penguin Books, 1980.

Joyce, James. *Ulysses*. New York: Modern Library, 1942.

Kesey, Ken. *One Flew Over the Cuckoo's Nest*. New York: Viking Press, 1962.

King, Stephen. *Carrie*. New York: Doubleday and Company, Inc., 1974.

———. *Different Seasons*. New York: Viking Press, 1982.

Kirst, Hans Hellmut. *Night of the Generals*. Translated by J. Maxwell Brownjohn. New York: Harper and Row, 1963.

Konigsburg, E. L. *A View from Saturday*. New York: Aladdin Paperback, 1999.

Koontz, Dean R. *How to Write Best Selling Fiction*. Cincinnati: Writer's Digest Books, 1981.

Lang, Andrew. *Custom and Myth*. London and New York: Longmans, Green, & Co., 1910.

Le Carré, John. *The Spy Who Came in from the Cold*. New York: Dell Publishing Co., 1965.

Lois Lowrey. *The Giver*. New York: Houghton Mifflin Co. 1993.

Mitchell, Margaret. *Gone With the Wind*. New York: The MacMillan Company, 1936.

Muller, Friedrich Max. *Comparative Mythology*. New York: Arno Press, 1977.

Nabokov, Vladimir. *Lolita*. New York: G. P. Putnam's Sons, 1955.

Patai, Raphael. *Myth and Modern Man*. Englewood Cliffs, N.J.: Prentice-Hall, Inc., 1972.

Puzo, Mario. *The Godfather*. New York: G. P. Putnam's Sons, 1969.

Raglan, Lord (FitzRoy Richard Somerset, Baron). *The Hero: A Study in Tradition, Myth, and Drama*. New York: Vintage Books, 1956.

Rice, Anne. *A Cry to Heaven*. New York: Alfred Knopf, 1982.

Shakespeare, William. *The Complete Works of Shakespeare*. Edited by George Lyman Kittredge. Boston: Ginn and Co., 1936.

Stowe, Harriet Beecher. *Uncle Tom's Cabin*. New York: Harper Collins, 1987.

Tolstoy, Leo. *Anna Karenina*. Translated by Constance Garnett et al. New York: Modern Library, 1994.

———. *War and Peace*. Translated by Constance Garnett. New York: Modern Library, 1994.

Travern, B. *Treasure of the Sierra Madre*. New York: Hill and Wang, 1967.

Woolf, Virginia. *Mrs. Dalloway*. New York: Harcourt, Brace and Co., 1925.